MW01231501

The Middle-Age of Aquarius

Barry Parham

ISBN: 1461006503
ISBN-13: 978-1461006503

ALSO BY BARRY PARHAM

Why I Hate Straws
An offbeat worldview of an offbeat world

Sorry, We Can't Use Funny

Blush
Politics and other unnatural acts

WHAT REVIEWERS ARE SAYING ABOUT BARRY PARHAM AND HIS FOURTH COLLECTION "THE MIDDLE-AGE OF AQUARIUS"

"A relentless wit … fresh, clever … laugh-out-loud material"

"Started laughing at the first sentence. Read it twice. Second paragraph had me laughing out loud."

"…so funny, so cynical…"

"I'm still in laughter-induced respiratory distress … incredibly funny"

"As many others have said … very, very funny … intelligently written"

"…fascinating and original…"

"Humorous, cynical and witty. A great book that made me laugh."

DEDICATION

To my siblings

To Kenneth: my brother by birth
To Diane: my sister by fortune
To Craig: part joyous angel, part jolly ox

TABLE OF CONTENTS

Get Your Zero-Trans-Fat Kicks on Route 66 **1**

The Middle-Age of Aquarius 3

Frijoles con Androgyny 9

Saint Funnel Cake & the Stallions 15

Pecan Pirates of the Pluff Mud 21

Home for the Hollow Days 27

Of (Mutant) Mice & Men (in Tights) 31

Slash & The Ghost 39

Snowblind 43

Fear & Self-Loathing **49**

The Zodiac Buzz-Killer 51

Abby Redux V 57

Pick a Number 63

National Weekday Month 69

Abby Redux VI 77

Comfortably Dumb 85

Abby Redux VII 91

How To Awesomefy Your Doppelganger 97

STUCK IN A J.O.B. WORKIN 4 D MAN OMG LOL **103**

Commuter Science 105

Airport Insecurity 113

Things To Not Say At Work 119

He Said WHAT? 125

Dear Santa: Send Lawyers, Guns & Money 131

Three Mittens For Tim's Cat 135

Who Ever Thought We'd Miss Nixon? 141

Uncle Sam, Inc. 143

Big Teeth 151

We, the Other People 157

Too Good To Be False 165

Courting the Zombie Caucus 171

How To Survive A Government Shutdown 175

Lame Duck Soup 183

We Are The Walrus 191

Ooh, Baby, It's A Wild World Wide Web 197

King Tut & the Cheeseheads 199

Santa Cops A Plea 205

Honey, Was That The Door? 211

A Salad for Samson 215

Life Irritates Art 221

Saint Clement Has Second Thoughts 227

Midnight in the Axis of Good and Evil 235

Setting Up Your Own Non-Prophet 243

PREFACE

Well, there I was, preparing to lob my fourth book at an unsuspecting world, when somebody suggested that I really ought to include a foreword or preface in the thing. I'm not sure why that suddenly needed doing; after all, I'd managed to publish my first three books without regard to any of the standard, normal book elements; you know, those niggling details that just tend to mire and crimp an author. Character development. Cohesion. Grammar. Plot and structure. Proofreading. Facts.

"But, don't you see," this somebody continued, "you need to let the reader know what the book is about. How is the reader supposed to know what the book is about?"

Okay. Fair enough. What's the book about? It's about fifteen bucks. So you could swap three copies of my book for almost a whole gallon of gas or, in South Florida, have two people killed. (three people, actually, unless they're very wide people)

But I can do much better than simply provide a description of what my book is about. I don't need to generalize or estimate. I can tell you with a certainty that this book is EXACTLY eight inches high.

As far as what's IN this book, I'll say this: you are, at this very moment, extremely close to reading a collection of weekly humor columns that lots of people say they find funny, though they could be lying. And that includes at least three people who are not members of my family, though they could be lying about that, too.

You are literally two or three page flips away from dipping into dozens of short essays about dating, dining, shopping, world events, pirates that love fast food, ghosts that hate chickens, Popeye vs. Samson, using alternate universes to get around a statute of limitations, ferrets, politicians (aka "tall ferrets") - you know, that sort of thing.

So. "Buyer beware!" Which is the kind of useless remark that always reminds me of one of my favorite ancient Nordic proverbs, "Ab svidden il ood perdnyek svidden ubn" which, roughly, translates into English as "I can eat more goose when my hip is not swollen."

I didn't say it was a *relevant* proverb. I just said I liked it.

Get Your Zero-Trans-Fat Kicks on Route 66

** Are you kidding me? A *drug trip*? Without a GPS? **

The Middle-Age of Aquarius

(Yeah, I know. "Flower adult" doesn't exactly roll off the tongue, does it?)

Last night, while I was asleep, I bench-pressed a shrimp boat, beat two dozen bad guys to death (with the boat), and fell off a mountain. At least, I guess that's what happened. Because that would help explain how, sometime during the night, I managed to damage my back.

It's very disappointing. After all, over the many years, so many sureties have ultimately proved undependable. But I thought I could still count on at least one thing: I almost never screw up while I'm asleep. Almost never. (Daylight, of course, is a whole different story.)

But last night, it happened. I woke up, sat up, and let out a manly yelp as some giant invisible wrench-wielding auto mechanic mistook my Latissimus dorsi for a loose lug nut.

This kind of nonsense didn't used to happen! This was not part of the plan, back when I was eighteen, immortal, and had just the one chin. I used to run ten, twenty miles, and that before breakfast. Now I need to get a good head start just to run a bath.

What happened? And when, exactly? I used to be acceptably attractive, or at least minimally hideous. Now I have Presbyopia and bifocal-induced nose dents. Now I have eyebrow dandruff. Lately, I have to make a tactical plan just to tackle a spiral staircase. These days, I have to think through, in advance, the necessary schematics that will allow me to bend over and then stand back up in the same day. And, for some reason, I now have horizontal hairs spoking out of my ears, like midget neck bolts on some fledgling Frankenstein.

What happened? We used to stay up till dawn; these days, I struggle to stay awake till dark. And now it's not even safe to nod off? Lovely. I lay me down to sleep, I perform some nocturnal Herculean feat, some mega-macho maneuver like, oh, rolling over too abruptly into a pillow divot, and I wake up all Quasimodo.

But even on the best of mornings, it now takes me a little lead time to attain any public-ready level of presentable humanity. My initial pre-caffeine walk from bed to bath looks like one of those pictorial school posters of man's evolutional stages, from knuckle-walking ape to fully upright used car salesman.

Maybe society's to blame; after all, in our current culture, personal responsibility is just so out of vogue, isn't it? Tasteless. Gauche.

So let's blame something else, like society. Not exactly hard to do. I mean, look around. We have 175 million TV channels. We have streaming books and music and movies so we don't have to go out, emails and webcams so we don't have to go visit. You can order groceries, prescriptions and penance, clothes and cars, appliances and spouses and salvation, all online. You're penalized if you work, but subsidized if you don't.

We are becoming inert. Homo stasis.

Case in point: the last time I bought a car, I had a custom car stereo installed. And the custom system came with ... ready? ... a remote control.

That's just wrong.

A remote control. For the radio in my car. Don't think about that for too long, else your ears will start bleeding. Or growing hair.

Face it, flower chirren. We've simply reached an age where the rules have changed (or, if you prefer, have been dumbed down). These days, personal victories consist of a list of things you've managed to *stop* doing (smoking, drinking beer from holes punched in the bottom of the can, wearing pants with holes in the knees, drinking in some frat-hole until you end up on your knees, flicking a lighter and yelling "Free Bird" whenever you're confronted with live music).

Some of you younger guys won't understand. You won't get it. Yet. It'll take you a while to catch on ... to get the memo ... to learn that it's not, in fact, wicked cool to open a conversation by bantering in Who-Got-More-Sick-This-Weekend comparative contests.

It took me a while.

See, I was born a long time ago, in the late 1950s. People don't realize how long ago that was. The year I was born, there were still only forty-eight states, although we were already getting a little tired of Arizona. Gas cost about thirty cents a gallon, and thin, nondescript men named Jake would pump it for you, *and* clean your windshield, *and* hit on your sister. All the "stooges" and "rascals" were still in Hollywood, instead of in Congress. There were still only two genders. There were just three TV stations, and there had only been eleven "Die Hard" sequels.

There was no Internet. Imagine that! In those days, if you wanted to get your identity stolen, you had to go outside!

Now, of course, we have the Internet - history's largest collection of untamed, unedited information, a staggering suppository of data which, according to mathematical theorists, may contain as many as three actual facts.

(Yes, I know. No, I did *not* intend to say "depository.")

The Internet also opens up some promising new vistas for those guys who are stuck in that nebulous "neither here nor there" limbo, that middle-age mesa between Metrosexual and Medicare. For example, there are hundreds of targeted Facebook ads begging your attention, all featuring nearly-clothed professional contortionists who are desperately seeking the companionship of guys over fifty.

No, they're not. They're desperately seeking the companionship of the *wallets* of guys over fifty.

You've seen their pictures, these confused coeds whose legs begin just beneath their air-brushed armpits, painfully posed as if they had dropped something on the floor, right in front of the camera, just after having undergone a Mick Jagger lip implant. According to the targeted Facebook ads, this lithe young Shiva, Destroyer of Egos and Champion of Pre-Nups, is staring longingly at you, virtually whispering something in direct allusion to pages 87-92 of the Kama Sutra.

No, she's not.

Don't kid yourself, kid. Stay on the ship, Captain Rehab.

She's not staring longingly at *you*. She's staring at the side of your jowly head, wondering with some concern if that wavy thing is an advance Recon unit from an extra-galactic mother-ship, scouting our planet in advance of a humanity-ending alien invasion.

Or just an errant ear hair.

Frijoles con Androgyny

(Indignation, indigestion, invisible women: could this be love?)

Every day, thousands of people walk up to me and ask, "How do you fi..."

Okay, that's not entirely true.

Often, people will walk up to me and a...

Okay, that's not true, either.

All right. Once, a guy I know asked me, "How do you find stuff to write about every week?"

True story. And it's a fair question, too, because people who know me know that I don't do anything. I don't like crowds. I hate flying. I like a book, an album, a warm fire, some Mexican food. If I could get Mexican food delivered, I'd never leave my house.

But occasionally, I'll put on the minimally-acceptable number of socially-required pieces of clothing necessary to go to a store, or to a concert, or to get some Mexican food. Or I'll pop out to visit with friends, who will inevitably ask me, "How do you find stuff to write about every week?" Or I'll motor away to spend some quality time with my parents, who will inevitably ask me to "please take some of this fruit home."

At my parents' home, in the town where I (more or less) grew up, there are always boxes and crates and cartons of fresh fruit. I don't know why that is, but they seem quite comfortable constantly navigating between pallets of grapefruit and tangelos, so I don't ask. Plus, there's practically zero chance of my parents ever getting scurvy.

Anyway, during a recent trip to visit them, I went out to eat with my parents. It was a mild mid-December early evening, a lovely occasion to visit a nice restaurant, and the three of us were to be joined by my cousin, Amber.

Amber, my cousin, is a good man and a good friend, and his name is not Amber. Calling a normal, healthy man "Amber" is, I've discovered, one of the singular advantages to writing fiction, though it carries the unfortunate side-effect that relatives may block your incoming phone calls. It may also explain why I don't get out much.

Maybe that's what's up with all the fruit. Perhaps my parents have convinced themselves that my condition could be cured, if conscientiously attacked by enough citrus.

But back here in our story about dinner, let's peek forward in time a bit, to the shank of the evening. It will surprise no one to hear that, for dinner on this evening, I angled toward anything at all that was Mexican, or Tex-Mex, or just simply hot. A blackened tuna steak, a mango and pepper salsa, garlic potatoes, a brimming bowl of black beans and onions. Ticket stamped. Barry happy.

And what happened *after* the meal may surprise no one, either, but it sure surprised *me*.

The four of us, there at table, were doing what all Americans do at nice restaurants, in that awkward limbo period that oscillates between the food being consumed, and the plates being gathered and cleared away. And so, as we each idly drew little rambling circles in our plates with our forks, our waiter, Lolita, approached and addressed me, directly.

"Sir, may I ask you a question?"

My eyes narrowed. I was trying to remember where I'd parked, and if I might ever have met the waiter's mom. "No. Or. Yes, I mean. Yes. What?"

"How were the black beans?"

In my little single guy skull, little warning gastro-klaxons fired, re-fired, and fired again. I stared at the waiter. Amber stared at my parents. My parents stared at the remaining black beans.

"Uh, um." I bartered for time. "Fine, they, uh. Fine. Why, um, would, why. Why, why would you ask?"

"Oh, nothing. Cook asked me to ask. New on the menu, I guess."

"Should I wor..."

Our waiter torpedoed for the kitchen.

"Well, that was odd," I began, trying to initiate a quick, empathic, internal-organ roll call. "Normally, you don't ge..." I paused, noting the approach of a smiling shift manager.

"Hi folks! Hope you're enjoying your meal with us! Just wondering ... how were the black beans?"

And people ask me how I find stuff to write about every week.

Anyway, back to the evening's pre-shank.

Amber was running a bit late, so my parents and I had ourselves seated at a nice four-top, with a nice view of the inevitable wall-mounted coats-of-arms and the federally-mandated restaurant aquarium. Shortly, we were approached by what I could only assume was our waiter's child.

Man, I'm getting old. The waiter - I'll call him "Lolita" - looked to be about twelve minutes shy of a massive puberty outbreak.

"Hello, gentlemen," chirped Lolita. "My name's Lolita, at least in this story, and I'll be your waiter-or-waitress tonight. Can I start you gentlemen off with something from the bar?" Lolita then whipped out a stubby crayon and wrote his or her name, backwards and upside-down, which was a pretty cool trick for a girl whose voice hadn't even changed yet.

Suddenly, it dawned on Lolita that my mother was at table, too, which is a handy discovery for a waiter to make. Step one: count the guests. Step two: spell "a t i l o L" upside-down with a crayon.

Clever of her or him to notice.

"I'm sorry, ma'am, I didn't see you there."

"Perhaps the pencil was in the way," I quipped, virtually guaranteeing myself top billing in my mother's future estate planning.

Lolita took note of our drink requests, then nodded at the empty seat next to me. "Do you know what she'd like to drink?"

"Lolita, I don't, in fact, know what she'd like to drink," I admitted. "To be honest, I didn't even know that he was a she."

Lolita, now totally discombobulated, turned smartly on his heel, and she beat a retreat to the safety of the kitchen, or perhaps to either one public bathroom or the other.

Poor kid. Wait till Amber shows up, and Lolita discovers I'm dating my cousin.

Saint Funnel Cake & the Stallions

(Horses in a hockey rink. What could go wrong?)

This week, because my nieces wanted to, I went to see the Royal Lipizzaner Stallions at a local arena, where we witnessed something simply amazing: nine beautiful horses that, for nearly two hours, did not "go to the bathroom."

Now, in the spirit of full disclosure, let me say that I don't like to get sued. So, in the spirit of not liking to get sued, let me say that the Royal Lipizzaner show is an outstanding entertainment that proudly represents a major historical contribution to the rich tapestry that is Europe. And when you're stuck for two hours in an enclosed space with nine enormous warrior animals, it's a bit of a blessing that they're enormous warrior animals that are also house-broken.

But America and Europe have always had different attitudes about, well, let's call it personal aroma ("l'odeur de corps"). Even today, you can walk along most any Parisian street ("rue") and get absolutely blinded ("rendre aveugle") by someone's, well, let's call it aura ("le funk"). It's as if they were hiding their own personal paper mill. It's like a live thing, a thing that wants out, a thing that could suddenly annex Poland, or vastly improve Detroit.

To be fair, it was quite a show. The Lipizzaner Stallions have been touring the world for forty-one years now, which, as I'm sure you'll agree, is a really long time between bathroom breaks ("le colostomy"). The show revolves around a presentation of "dressage," which is French for "Imaginary Horse Tutu." But though perfected in Europe, dressage was mentioned as far back as 400 B.C. by the Greek historian and military leader, Xenophon (literal translation: marimba).

Dressage includes many amazing elements, including the Walk, the Lope, the Eddie Cantor, the Galumph, and the Trotsky (literal translation: small trot). One of the more fascinating maneuvers involves the rider commanding the horse to walk briskly, without actually going anywhere (literal translation: filibuster).

(Don't quote me on this, but if I heard the emcee correctly, there's another maneuver known as the "extended trots." I'll move on. I have way *too many immature male genes inside for me to loiter in this paragraph, thinking up jokes.)*

As the evening continued, though, things grew increasingly interesting. I realized that dressage is a lot like a formal state dinner in Washington. Big on form, small on substance. Each participant announced with great fanfare. Each participant arriving from (and eventually returning to) a plush, coddled life largely funded by other people's money. Lots of prancing about, lots of public drooling.

Dressage here, politics there. Red carpet here, red carpet there. White horse here, white house there. Imaginary horse tutus here, self-policing ethics committees there. Overdressed people with whips here ... see what I mean?

The bubbly emcee of the show, whom I'll call "Paolo," provided a running commentary (see "extended trots"). Paolo proved to be an entertaining mix of host, historian, carnival barker, and open-mike-night comedian. And Paolo did inform, introducing me to several previously unknown facts. For instance, I did not know that 60% of a horse's weight is borne by the front legs, unlike, say, a kangaroo, or Paris Hilton.

On this night, the arena itself (a hall most often utilized for ice hockey) was nearly empty. But the last time I was here (again, because my nieces wanted to), we had come to watch a Monster Truck rally, and the place was packed to the rafters. So I don't know exactly why the Lipizzaner show failed to draw. Maybe because of very cold weather. Maybe the night was yet another victim of the "worst American economy since last week's worst American economy." Maybe the promoters should think about staging a tag-team wrestling event, a cage match, pitting the stallions against the Monster Trucks.

(If you've never attended a Monster Truck rally, it's just a big, unbelievably loud anger management seminar where people purge pent-up aggression by destroying several dozen cars and trucks. Basically, it's just like being in the parking lot of a South Florida deli when the retirement home crowd arrives for Sunday brunch, but with fake skulls staring out the back window. Plus, at a Monster Truck rally, they take turns.)

Now, in the spirit of *still* not liking to get sued, even ten or twelve paragraphs later, let me say that this local arena is an outstanding entertainment venue that proudly represents a major historical contribution to the rich tapestry that is not Europe (though it sometimes smells the same). Also, it seems to be heavily involved in the trafficking of smuggled holy relics.

If you're planning a visit, you should know that this venue serves bottled holy water. At least, I assume it's holy water, given the price they're asking, with a straight face, for a bottle of the stuff. The arena also hawks holy popcorn, blessed beer, and (again, based on the price) a variety of possibly unleavened funnel cake that can trace its lineage directly back to the first Passover.

(*I noticed a kiosk selling hot dogs, too, but they were unable to complete my credit check before the show began.*)

For two hours, the horses performed, and were perfect. Elegant, exquisite, perfect animals. Their riders, likewise. But I couldn't help worrying about the ticket holders who had been seated in the front row. At many points during the evening, they were literally within inches of these parading, magnificent beasts, with their magnificent necks, and their magnificent ability to drool and slobber like Winston Churchill on a three-day brandy binge. Sitting on that front row would have been just like being too close to the stage at a Gallagher concert.

One more interesting factoid: did you know that all that drooling and slobbering is considered a Lipizzaner asset? So says Paolo. In a Lipizzan, it's a sign of good breeding. In my neighborhood, it's a sign of someone who survived an accident involving a large farm implement.

And after sharing that little Lipizzanian tidbit, Paolo smoothly segued into another joke, this one about drooling ("le phlegm").

According to Paolo, a favorite expression around the Lipizzaner community is this: "Spit happens."

And the arena erupted in a non-deafening wall of thick, utter silence. The place turned into a tomb.

(Note to Paolo: When performing in the Bible Belt, eighty-six the "Spit happens" sketch.)

Pecan Pirates of the Pluff Mud

(You are now entering South Carolina. Got rogues?)

For those of you who've not yet visited, coastal South Carolina is an amazingly beautiful place. But there's a downside: to get to the South Carolina coast, at some point you have to drive through South Carolina.

Part of the problem is its location. South Carolina has freeways that connect irritated people from the northern States with irritated people from Florida. This means that our highways are an endless Mad Max outtake, a road rage arena of alien people, all in a hurry to get somewhere else.

First, there's the north-bound group, the hot, hurried, "had enough" hordes exiting Florida for various, often legal, reasons. This group includes:

- Shell-shocked vacationers, irritated because they just blew their entire Everglades holiday crouched in a damp unlit hotel room, hiding from three escaped pet Burmese pythons and eleven unscheduled hurricanes, all named Bob.
- Family Patriarchs captaining their Family Vacation Vehicles, irritated because, during the previous, intense six-hour

period, they just spent over twenty-one hundred dollars on twelve speeding tickets in south Georgia, a money-sucking black hole estimated to be the single largest continuous speed trap in the known universe.

- Relocating registered sexual predators, irritated because they grew so prevalent in Florida that they were forced to join a union and file papers of incorporation, and they're now classified as "too big to fail."
- Indignant "undocumented workers," irritated because their Social Security checks were late, their free health care didn't include a free private hospital room, and they didn't get a free gym uniform with their free in-state college tuition.
- Traveling citrus salesmen, irritated because a sudden outbreak of political correctness forced them to change their name from the "Indian" to the "Indigenous Disenfranchised Proud Culturally-Significant North American Human Beings" River Fruit Company.
- Patois-spewing drug couriers, irritated because, unlike in Florida, all the traffic signs in South Carolina are printed in English.
- Retirement-age Republican "snowbirds," irritated because they've still got a really long way to drive, and they no longer own a colon.

And then, heading south, all hopped up on freeway exit coffee, are the tourists and the Jews, eager to "experience" the "Deep South," to stand "in line" instead of "on line," hoping to grab a glimpse of "old times there that are not forgotten," or to get a photo of a "land's sake," or maybe a grit tree.

Now, personally, I don't know or care how to spot a southbound Jew in a car. But all my life I've been hearing, from my elders and from stand-up comics, that all Jews eventually go to Florida and wear white pants. And I always trust comics (although many of my elders have pretty much turned out to be full of "deep south").

This tourist fascination with "Dixie" has resulted in the establishment of an entire cottage industry, dedicated to marketing "quaint antebellum memorabilia" (literal translation: "incredibly trite garbage mass-produced in Taiwan"). Dotted along the off-ramps stuck to South Carolina's handful of freeways, there are approximately 247 billion shops, dives, joints and turn-offs, each selling "A Jim Nabors Christmas" CDs, several versions of salt-and-pepper shaker sets painted to look like Al Jolson, and a fatal foodstuff known as the "pecan log," a goo-laced mystery stick that is (to use the technical gastronomic term) pretty much full of "deep south."

Besides their uncanny uber-caramel ability to extract completely healthy adult molars, it turns out that pecan logs are the item most often stolen from freeway exit shops. Maybe people are just too embarrassed to purchase the foul things. Maybe there's some bizarre freeway contest going on, something larcenous bubbling just below the surface of normal society, some kind of sick citrus salesmen scavenger hunt. It's possible. Freeway exit coffee can have that kind of effect on a man.

Often, South Carolina freeway culture is a collision of worlds. Here's an overheard conversation at a restaurant counter, along an anonymous exit:

"Hey, honey. Wattle at bee?"
"Pardon?"
"What y'all eating, honey?"

"You guys got any hard rolls?"
"Naw, honey. All our bread's fresh."

But take any exit off the rod-straight 95 freeway in lower South Carolina and, within an hour, you'll be embraced by some of the most beautiful scenery imaginable.

And some of the most haunted, too. That's where I met Bessie, the ghost.

Okay, technically, I didn't *meet* Bessie. I met her portrait. I don't know how, technically, you *meet* a ghost, and I wouldn't know what to say if I did.

"Hi, Ghost."
"Human! Man, it's been a while since I saw one of you."
"Loved your portrait."
"Thanks. Hey! You got any hard rolls?"
"Pardon?"
"Forget it. Hey! Wanna play a game?"
"Uh, sure."
"Pull my finger ... off!"

But I know Bessie was a ghost, because her eyes followed me.

You know what I mean? Ever been alone in a room with one of those unsettling paintings of people whose painted eyes seem to watch you as you walk about the room? Ever had that tingly feeling? I don't mean that "mmm hmmm" glare they give you at the local IRS office, or at a freeway off-ramp that sells pecan logs, but that eerie feeling you get, left alone in the parlor of some ancient plantation home, with Jim Nabors echoing "rum pa pum pum" into the rafters.

The nice non-dead lady who was escorting me through this particular plantation told me that the little eyeball trick is actually a learned artistic technique known as the "Ubiquitous Gaze." See, long ago, before cell phone apps, people used to pay other people to paint "portraits," which were large drawings of angry people wearing exceptionally weird clothing and holding absurdly-heavy sharp objects, which may explain the anger. You've probably seen at least one portrait in your life: a famous one called the Mona Lisa. Not coincidentally, given that I'm talking "Ubiquitous Gaze" right now, the Mona Lisa is a classic example of "Ubiquitous Gaze," not to mention another, lesser-known technique known along the freeway exits of medieval Europe as the "Mocking Smirk."

During my plantation visit, I learned that painters who created "Gazers" employed a technique quite common to the Trompe l'Oeil school of painting (literal translation: "trick the eye"), a term derived from the ancient French expression "l'oeil tromper." (literal translation: "Nice trick! I surrender.")

See, long ago, Trompe l'Oeil was quite popular, because there were no cell phone apps. The main goal of Trompe l'Oeil was to create something that made people sit around, stare at stuff, and wonder: is it real or is it painted? Which undoubtedly led to gripping conversations like this:

"Your thoughts, Comte?"
"Oh, I just can't tell!"
"Mademoiselle, your turn."
"My turn, what?"
"Yon object. It is real, or it is a painting?"
"You're kidding, right?"

"Come, mademoiselle, indulge us. Play our little game."
"Well, Knickers Boy, let's see. It's in a frame, nailed to a wall. There's *one* clue."
"Le smirk!"

According to another ubiquitous entity known as Google, the Ubiquitous Gaze technique is "an effect of perspective" (not that we need to drag politics into this) and asking a painter to do up the old relative's head shot in a U-Gaze was quite an expensive request, which means that ancient people used to pay extra out-of-pocket money to get pictures to stare *back* at you, which means that ancient people were (to use the technical gastronomic term) stupid.

On the other hand, to be fair to ancient people, our current crop of non-dead people purchase pecan logs.

Or not.

Maybe they should get some Gazers at the freeway exits, to keep an eye on those citrus salesmen.

Home for the Hollow Days

(From candy corn to candied yams to candy canes. America.)

Okay. The Thanksgiving holiday season is officially over. And we all know what *that* means. It's finally time for me to get busy, doing exactly what millions of you are busily doing.

Yep. It's time for me to talk about Halloween.

I know. It's a bit late to get around to anything involving Halloween. I know. By now, I ought to be outside, precariously balancing on a ladder, turning my house's gutters into a traffic-stopping festival of malfunctioning miniature light-bulbs. I ought to be outdoors, tastefully decorating my lawn with Biblically-relevant pre-formed plastic statues of Walt Disney's dwarves, Peruvian-looking wise men and radioactive deer. I ought to be on the Internet, trying to figure why some people say "creche" when they mean "nativity scene." I ought to be on my knees, honoring the true meaning of Christmas: free shipping.

I know. I'm late. But, in my own defense: I, like our lame duck Congress, had a lot of work to do.

Unlike Congress, I got mine done.

I don't know if this Congress actually has a duck, but they sure are lame. I did apply for my own "lame duck" permit, but since Congress forgot to pass a budget, all government offices are currently closed. Maybe they're hoping Santa Claus will bring them a budget.

Santa was planning to just give everybody in Congress a lump of coal, but he was stymied after an injunction of estoppel was filed by an activist group of pro-clean-energy environmentalist elves, the North Pole Workers Local #8 (not to be confused with the Vegas Pole Workers Local #42D).

I hate it when Santa gets estopped.

I'm kidding, of course. I'm not here to talk about Halloween. Besides, Halloween's no fun anymore, at least not in my neighborhood. First of all, none of the occasionally-short people who look to me to feed their candy monkey are *from* my neighborhood. This isn't games and good fun: this is a nocturnal guerilla incursion, calling for facial recognition software. It's nearly dark, there are small strangers standing in my yard, they're all demanding food, and I don't know who they are.

And call me old-fashioned, but I just can't get used to handing out candy to a "child" who drives up in his own car.

When did the trick-or-treat rules change? What's the current cutoff age these days for Halloween? Eligibility to drive? Voter registration? AARP membership? This Halloween, I entertained several candy-requesting visitors who were taller than I. They don't even bother with masks or costumes anymore, unless those eyebrow piercings I saw were purchased as part of a "Disturbed Valley Girl" costume pack at Target (to me, they looked more like part of a Rodent Eradication kit from Terminex). One trick-or-treater had a full-arm-length dragon tattoo. One offered me a smoke. I didn't know if I should be handing out candy or condoms.

And this year, there's a whole new group of "children" who are either speaking a completely foreign language, or who are collectively participating in a shared psychotic episode. I don't know *what* they're saying, so I don't say a word: I just smile and lob candy. I'm afraid to respond to their unfamiliar chatter, or make gestures, or point, or even nod. For all I know, they're selling vinyl siding, or asking me if I would be interested in a mail-order Russian bride, or running for Congress.

I particularly remember one little cherub who came by. He was, I don't know, forty-four inches tall, tops. He wore an eye patch, a black robe and a white cape, and he sported one of those knitted, multi-pointy, jingly jester caps. You know the ones. He looked like a short snowboarding excommunicated stunt-nun after a bad "black diamond" accident.

This stumpy little waif snobbishly scanned my bowl of candy with a critical eye (his good eye), and I swear I heard him snort. Then he pointed and told *me* which pieces of my pelf he preferred.

"Pfff. Not *that*," he scoffed. "Gimme *those*."

I scanned my yard and the curb, making sure there were no nearby grown-ups looking, or any lawyers poised to estop me.

For a second, just a brief moment, I entertained a little fantasy involving this manners-challenged munchkin, a favorable breeze and a football tee.

But the mood passed. I blinked, cleared my head, smiled and replied, "No problem, young sir! Now off to bed with you, and remember: don't smoke! Smoking could stunt your growth! Oops! Too late! *Ha ha ha!*"

And then, of course, I tripped him on his way down the steps. Hey, it's *good* for the ungrateful little candy snatcher. Adversity. Builds character.

He'll need it when he runs for Congress.

Of (Mutant) Mice & Men (in Tights)

(The Nutcracker Suite: what your parents didn't tell you)

All right, then. YOU decide.

I'll say it again: the "Nutcracker Suite" ballet, which, over time, has become a Christmas tradition, is a sick, twisted journey into psychotropic drub aguse. Sorry, I meant to say drug abuse. See, it's still haunting me.

We have no business subjecting young, impressionable children to this stuff, particularly after we've already plumped the kids full of sweets, candy and egg nog, and then told them not to peek while an old, hairy, obese guy, wearing red felt and black go-go boots, slips down the chimney and starts handing out free Wii consoles.

Doubters, are you? All right, then.

YOU decide.

The now-famous "Nutcracker" music, which was written by Peter Bogdanovich Tchaikovsky (or maybe it was Paddy Chayefsky), was based on "The Nutcracker and the King of Mice," a story written by a German fellow named E.T.A. Hoffman, who later invented airport flight delays.

Unlike some authors, E. "Dustin" Hoffman took up writing later in life. His first career, as a pest-control expert with Das Orkin Uber Alles, ended badly following an unfortunate rodent-related incident in the nearby hamlet of Hamelin.

Yes, rodents. Coincidence?

In what may have been a further foreshadowing of things to come, there were young impressionable children involved there in Hamelin, too, not to mention a roving mercenary woodwind artist named Pied.

Although the "Nutcracker" story's details have changed over the years, as eyewitnesses eventually were laid down or sobered up, the basic plot remains the same. And it remains a disturbing jaunt through a disturbed mind, a maddened maze of mice and imaginary men, of makeshift tourniquets and massive tooth decay.

The central character of the "Nutcracker" story is a young, very hairy German girl named Fur Elise. Among other bad youthful decisions, Fur gets mixed up with some gypsies from the opera "Carmen," which was a constantly looming danger back in ancient times, especially in years that began with "ye olde." The gypsies tease Fur until she agrees to partake of some tea made of psilocybin truffles, after which she lapses into a candy-laced dream about a magical wooden Nutcracker formerly known as

Prince, who promises to take Fur Elise to an enchanted place where they'll "party like it's ye olde 1999."

Sadly, their travel plans are delayed due to the Nutcracker's fierce battle against a Mouse King with seven heads (many of them played by Arlen Specter). Eventually, though, Prince overcomes the King's album sales, then drags Fur Elise around the European club circuit, where she basically sits and fumes while "Mr. Sensitivity" is entertained by successive groups of nearly-clad women.

Sick stuff, this.

Still doubting, are you? Okay, let's review the story in detail. As Act I begins, a bunch of rich people are ramping up for a wild party.

Mmm hmm. This is what, in Fairy Tale Analysis school, they call a "clue."

It's Christmas Eve at the compound of the ruthless Stahlbaum truffle cartel. The Stahlbaums (literal translation: Scarface) are hosting their annual Border Mule Appreciation party, and for some reason, their children, Fur Elise and Onde Fritz, are getting along. (Right there, you know drugs are involved.) The kids are dancing and playing, occasionally playfully poking each other in the eyes.

Guests arrive, a lot of bowing and ye olde high-fiving goes on, and everyone takes note of which loser-fraus are wearing the same tired outfits they wore at Thanksgiving.

Suddenly, a Godfather named Oscarmeyer appears at the door, not realizing he's in the wrong movie. Oscarmeyer is not only a major player in the Teutonic Mafia (literal translation: more than one tonic), he's also a skilled clock-maker, a gifted toy-maker and effectively lethal at close range. Swiftly getting into the party spirit, he pulls out two blazing automatic weapons and the head of a guest's prize racehor ...

No, sorry. Wrong movie.

Oscarmeyer pulls out two life-size dolls which begin to dance ... on their own, mind you, they begin to dance ... and everybody calmly watches these two lifeless toys self-animate and dance around the compound. None of the guests collapse, shrieking in madness; nobody runs out of the room babbling for the police, or for some nearby exorcism-enabled Lutheran.

The mood is set. As the attending adults grow ever more inured to bizarre behaviors, they begin unwrapping and re-swapping Pajama-Gram gift boxes, trading Frank Zappa quotes, and thumbing through the Stahlbaum's pre-DVD collection of Quentin Tarentino DVDs (Johannes Gutenberg edition).

Huddled around the Christmas tree, the kids are keeping busy enjoying a game of Checkers, making playing pieces using tablets from their Ritalin prescriptions. In a grand flourish, Oscarmeyer presents his holiday presents to Fur Elise and Onde Fritz. Fur is given a stiff, attractive nutcracker whose solitary skill is that its mouth moves. (Oddly, given nothing but that single talent, it will one day manage to get itself elected President of the United States and win the Nobel Peace Prize.)

Onde Fritz gets some kind of lame, bobo bugle. Unimpressed, and out of Ritalin, he develops a marked tic in his left eye, grabs his sister's Nutcracker, and snaps it in half.

Fur Elise is heartbroken. (She's also furiously homicidal, in a howling, Stephen-King-character, blinding-black-rage kind of way. But mostly, heartbroken.) Happily, Oscarmeyer is able to quickly repair the Nutcracker by plugging its injury with billions of taxpayer dollars he magically draws from the air.

The adult guests finally reach a glazed level of shared over-medication and begin to drift out the front door and toward ye olde SUVs. Onde Fritz and two other truants grab some matches and head upstairs, muttering something about "Oscarmeyer" and "effigy." Fur Elise grabs the Nutcracker, gulps from a nearly adult beverage, and falls asleep.

Round midnight, Fur notices that the Christmas tree seems to be growing taller, and she shouts "Ich bin ein Berliner!" (literal translation: "Whoa. That's, like, trippy, dude!") The wall clock seems to be melting into a magic ring. Keanu Reeves runs down a wall and convinces her to eat the correct pill, and then an invisible cat grins and offers her a chaser of Pulp Fiction Orange Juice (starring John Travolta as Samuel Jackson). Next, the room is filled with an army of mice, led by their leader, King Specter.

Offstage, we hear a markedly non-liturgical litany, as Oscarmeyer discovers and then stomps out his own effigy.

Suddenly, the Nutcracker Prince blows a bugle, awakening a Mr. Potato Head and two animated avatars who sound just like Tom Hanks and Tim Allen. They all advance on a box of toy soldiers, conscript them, and immediately forget to not invade England.

The Mouse King captures the Nutcracker and forces him to rebuild the Japanese economy, using counterfeit petro-dollars and the business analytical techniques from some consultant named Deming.

Fur Elise, realizing that the First Act is nearly over, whips off an open-toed shoe and heaves it at the Mouse King, hitting him squarely on heads two, five, and six. The Mouse King drops to the floor and the mice run away, dragging their leader's body along, in hopes of restoring the King's big-headed body once multiple-skull skull fractures are covered by Universal Health Care, sometime around ye olde 2014.

Now that there's no longer any danger of anybody hitting him, the Nutcracker claims the whole ballroom as his kingdom, invades France, and demands that no one shall operate the TV remote control but him.

And then came Intermission. (literal translation: How Can Chocolate-Covered Peanuts Cost Twenty-Seven Dollars?)

After the lights dim, the Nutcracker transports Fur Elise to a pre-Super Bowl party in The Land of A-Recreational-Drug-Often-Referred-To-As-Snow (starring Johnny Depp as the Mosquito Coast Mule and Al Pacino as Miami Beach).

Once their appetites return, the couple rolls on to visit The Land of Sweets, where they're scheduled to have a mid-psychotic-episode conference with the Sugar Plum Fairy; however, Sugar can't take a meeting right now because she's busy negotiating a hostile takeover of Tooth Fairy, Inc. Sugar has them wait in her outer office for hours. After some frenzied phone calls, Sugar scores some comp festival tickets for her guests, so Fur and the

Nutcracker ultimately kill the afternoon at the United Nations, watching the General Assembly perform some dances (literal translation: non-binding resolutions). First, there's the Spanish, then the Arabians, the Russians, the Chinese, the Mirliton, the Waltz of th...

WHOA. Hold up. The Mirliton?

Yes. The Mirliton: a giant gingerbread house named Mother Ginger barges on-stage and, without even a "Hello sailor," rips off her Velcro-prepped skirt.

And naturally, in the world of E.T.A. Hoffman, eight little gingerbread children live under there.

The little ginger-kinder jiggle and dance, though, oddly, they never hold up any "HELP ME" signs or make a sudden break for the border, or the Lutheran exorcist in the wings.

Mmm hmm. And we Americans thought WE had a housing crisis.

Why "mirliton?" Good question. According to our friend, Mr. Internet Search, a mirliton is a pear-shaped vegetable, or a chayote squash, or a comic book cat, or a kazoo, or a festival in New Orleans. And so, for blisteringly obvious reasons, this little slice of Tchaikovsky's late-night indigestion has managed to get itself manifested as the Dance of the Mirlitons.

Now, after the Mirliton dance is over, the cookie-based kiddies file back under Mother Ginger's skirt, making it look like the gingerbread is eating the children, a disturbing image which is enough to put you right off your chocolate-covered raisins.

Next, as I recall the plot - and I don't - some flowers dance a waltz, but by now, the audience is beginning to question sanity and some other cosmic fundamentals. So it's frankly a bit of an anticlimax when Sugar Plum eighty-sixes the Tooth Fairy and installs her own Chief Operating Officer (Psychosis Division), the handsome, spandex-sporting Cavalier (literal translation: Sugar Plum's sister's boy). Sugar and the Cavalier dance a beautiful pas de deux (literal translation: more than one pas).

Finally, because the theatre was only booked for two hours, Fur Elise wakes up from a diabetic coma. She's under the tree, cradling the Nutcracker, nursing a hammering headache, and missing a shoe. And as Oscarmeyer dials Child Protective Services, the curtain falls and we fade to black.

And for some reason, the audience is absolutely STARVING.

Slash & The Ghost

(Barbecue, boredom and bird therapy. Another day in South Carolina.)

This past weekend, I took a trip to the South Carolina coast (an area known to South Carolina locals as The Lowcountry) in order to sign some books. They weren't my books or anything - I just like to sign books. And when you're wired for a weird habit like that, it's best to slip out of town before you feed your monkey.

So, on a bright Friday morning, I left my hometown of Creyer (pronounced "Cur"), a lovely small town near the Blue Ridge Mountains in northwest South Carolina (an area known to South Carolina locals as The Upstate), angling for The Lowcountry. I've written to you before about Creyer. It's an increasingly eager little town with a serious annexation addiction, a growth-mad little burg whose motto seems to be "If you lay sewer pipe, they will come."

I aimed my car downhill, towards the middle of the state (an area known to South Carolina locals as The Middle Of The State), driving southbound along a recently-refurbished connector freeway that exists to assist in connecting the South Carolina Upstate with the rest of the state, and it is a freeway that quite obviously exists for no other reason, including aesthetics. This is not a road designed for ooh-ing and aah-ing and photo ops and excited finger-pointing. This is a road designed for drone-like concentration, for ennui, for bathos, for catatonia. It was apparently built (and lately rebuilt) with a very long ruler, very much money, and absolutely no sense of humor whatsoever. This connector has been resurfaced in a bright white concrete motif and it has the distinction of being the only manmade object visible from outer space that is also insanely boring.

Here's how desolate it is: the entire project is some forty-odd miles of pipe-straight pavement, and along that endless, lined layer of laser, there are only eighteen McDonald's. That may be a McDonald's-free-zone world record. I'm talking deep-space desolate. At mile marker thirty-two, I saw an armadillo clutching a tiny envelope with the single, sad, scribbled word, "Goodbye." The thunderingly mind-numbed animal had committed suicide.

Approximately two hours and sixteen hundred McDonald's later, I drove into the city of Columbia, the capitol of our state, a place where the primary civic activity is trying to not die on one of their fine freeways. There are other activities, of course, and there's no immediately obvious reason why the locals couldn't enjoy life like anyone else, anywhere else: after all, Columbia contains a major university, a military base and a state government, so residents clearly have easy access to drugs, beer, weapons and clowns.

Columbia is also famous for being the only metropolitan area in America that has more barbecue restaurants than it has McDonald's franchises. And by this point, you may be starting to gain an understanding of the suicidal nature associated with driving through Columbia. This kind of thing gets to you, pulls you under, tends to draw you down into a funk. It's no coincidence that, actuarially speaking, armadillos have virtually no life expectancy at all here.

Some uneventful hours later, I made it to The Lowcountry, where, in short order, I met a ghost named Bessie, a pit bull named Slash, and an unnamed trans-lesbian rooster that was intensely hated by its owner.

During my visit, I learned the fowl's sad story. Some time before, it seems, the rooster's owner had bought a bunch of "biddies." Or so she thought. Then one morning one of the "hens" started drinking beer, hogging the remote control, leaving the toilet seat up, and spending all Sunday afternoon watching football. Mrs. Owner realized she had a problem: a confused hen, a bi-biddy, a latent crower, a chick trapped in a dude's body.

So now, each morning after the noise lets up, Mrs. Owner shoos the rooster out into the street and then waits impatiently for an "unfortunate" accident, perhaps hoping that some visiting driver from Columbia, some hurried road warrior, distracted and spackled with an odd, pungent, mustard-based sauce, will rip through the neighborhood at Mach II or III and send the gender-jangled bird to join Bessie.

Bessie, I discovered, is the ghost that haunts a famous old Southern home in a famous old Southern historic district, on a plat situated just across the lane from Mrs. Owner (and within half a block of eleven McDonald's drive-thrus). According to the tales, Bessie was one of those capricious young people, those free spirits that used to be tolerantly referred to as a "handful" and are now judicially referred to as a "Paris Hilton." Bessie, apparently, never married and, apparently, never much missed the matrimonial experience, either.

The story of Slash, the pit bull, is too good a tale to co-star in some rogue rooster's story, so we'll have to meet again one day for that one. For now, suffice it to say that I met Slash when I was stuck in a small, disabled boat in the middle of the Calibogue Sound, a large body of McDonald's-franchise-free water that lies between Hilton Head and Daufuskie Islands, and my introduction to the pit bull, verbatim, went like this: "This is Slash. He bites."

By the way, I'm kidding, of course, about Mrs. Owner's rooster starting to drink beer one morning. Despite his/her/its barnyard orientation issues, the rooster was, as we say in South Carolina, "decent people." The rooster did not start drinking beer one morning; like anyone else, the rooster waited till after lunch to start drinking beer.

Well, anyone else except commuters in Columbia.

And I'm guessing Mrs. Owner would shell out big money to borrow Slash.

Snowblind

(Tips on how to not become Jack Nicholson during a blizzard)

It was the biggest winter storm to hit the American South in over three decades. And by the time sunshine and sanity finally glanced back down on the Southern landscape, a national holiday had gone missing, forests of Sliced White Bread trees had been slash-harvested, and greedy grocers had permanently disfigured 18,000 milk cows.

Yeah, yeah, yeah.

"Yeah, yeah, yeah" is the typical meteorological analysis of the typical Southern male, when confronted with news of a pending winter emergency. Partly, this is due to winter weather over-forecasting, which happens every year. But Southerners have learned to expect such from TV Weather Pros, people with names like Tiff or Carmelottinola or Bink, who refer to rain as a "rain event," and who stand in front of weather maps, totally blocking our states, while the blue parts of their Weather Pro clothes blink in and out of existence.

Southerners are also a bit numb to weather warnings because we get endless alerts about tornados and hurricanes which, unlike blizzards, visit the South on a regular basis, often before breakfast. And after. And during.

But let's face it: guys just don't do a whole lot of complex thinking or long-term planning. Consider how guys communicate at life's three major milestones - Birth, Matrimony and Death:

First words: "Goo goo. Pull my finger."
Marriage: "Hold on ... she was *how* old?"
Last words: "Hey, y'all. Watch this!"

ETYMOLOGICAL SIDEBAR: We now know that "goo goo" is early guy human for "Any chips left?"

But as it turned out, this was a real (and a really bad) snowstorm, at least by our balmy Southern standards. Here's how serious the weather situation was here in upstate South Carolina: in order to provide a seamless, endless flow of weather updates, the local TV station pre-empted the mid-morning's "Live with Regis"!

It might've gotten ugly. Such radical re-programming could have caused a civil backlash. Attacks on the thoughtless TV station, that sort of thing. Hordes of torch-carrying, Mom-Jeans-wearing Moms, storming out of the suburbs, so furiously angry that they turn into grainy, black & white film. Or things could've turned politically violent, especially if any of those insane, raging Republicans and sharp-fanged Tea Party psychotics started to rumble. Next thing you know, they might start ... now, hang on to something ... they might start reading stuff out loud, even atavistic documents with outdated concepts, like the U.S. Constitution, or the Bible.

But then, of course, the *real* madness began, as hundreds of thousands of simple idiots rushed the roads and descended upon the local grocers for whole milk and white bread. It's an unexplained, unavoidable trigger. Snow = Horde Whole Milk. Ice = Stock Up On White Bread. It's a constant in the Universe, like hydrogen, or Dick Clark. When winter weather threatens, people just instinctively stampede the grocers for bread, and for milk, including calcium-challenged families who haven't seen live teeth in their family dining room since Prohibition.

And since I, too, am a simple idiot, I skidded my way to the grocers, wondering if they would still have any food. Sheesh. They didn't even have any *carts*.

Things To Do During a Blizzard

- Eat. Especially cereal. Remember, there are now 361 gallons of milk in your fridge, and every carton has that ominous, looming "Curdle Date."
- This is very, very important. Whatever you do, whatever happens, no matter how stir-crazy you may get, absolutely do not watch "The Shining."
- But when you do (and because you're a guy, you will), watch it backwards. It's calming, in a claustrophobic, cabin fever kind of way, to watch Jack Nicholson backing out of hotel bedrooms, as he slowly goes sane.
- And while we're talking about Stephen King...
- If you live near a sewer grate, build a snowman's head that looks like Pennywise, Tim Curry's spooky clown character in the movie, "IT." Position the grinning snowman's head on the sewer grate, so it looks like the insane clown is staring

out from the sewer. Long-term, this has the additional advantage of drastically reducing visits from door-to-door salesmen. I've actually done this, during a snowstorm in another city, but eventually the neighbors made me move.

- Turn on the TV and watch Bill O'Reilly, but don't listen to him. Instead, mute the TV and cue up a playlist of Frank Sinatra albums. Then sit back and watch. Shortly, you'll start to experience this odd sensation, like you're in "Godfather II," or you've been granted a private audience with the Pope.
- Shovel your driveway, or scrape your car. Here's how prepared I was for seven-plus-inches of snow: after a couple of days, I stuttered my way to the curb to scrape the snow and ice off my car, using one of those plastic pinch clips that guys get for Christmas: those clips you keep in a kitchen drawer to manage half-eaten bags of potato chips. It got the de-icing job done, but at a dire cost: I lost the chips.
- Write the next great American novel. If you need a story idea, here's one (what with trying to finish all this milk before it expires, I'm not gonna be using it): a female NASCAR driver with massive "sweater assets" saves a Baptist bird-dog from being exported to China by gay Yankee vegetarians, by hitting them repeatedly with her King James version of the U.S. Constitution. Of course, happy endings are out of style these days, so our heroine then opens a specialty brasserie, which fails due to city council over-regulation. Working title: "The Crepes of Graft."

So, hang in there, stay busy, drink your milk (quickly), and don't try to drive in the ice, because *you don't know how to drive in the ice.* You can't do it. No, you can't. Yes, *you.*

If you're a female reading this, then you know him. You know good and well that he's sitting over there, right now, fixating like a chump on the mental image, "the heroine opened her specialty brasserie." Act. Act now. Hide the simple idiot's car keys ... *now* ... before you hear the dreaded Simple Idiot Death Warble:

"Hey, y'all. Watch this!"

And if you're of a mind, please help support the Sliced White Bread Reforestation Fund. It's tax-deductible!

So far.

Fear & Self-Loathing

** Free love wasn't, and self-help didn't **

The Zodiac Buzz-Killer

(The effects of salad dressing on the last 20,000 years)

In case you haven't heard, you're not you anymore. Nobody is who they were anymore, because after 23,000 years of just sitting around aligning all over the place, all the Zodiac stars have moved. This is the type of pronouncement that is known, in scientific circles, as "bone stupid."

See, according to very calm, flowing-robe-wrapped people with names like Tawny and Holar, the Zodiac is a system for defining who you are and how you act, based on where the stars were on your birth day. The Zodiac was formed 23,000 years ago, at 4:12 on a Thursday afternoon, by invisible energy auras that regularly speak to Tawny and Holar. This is the type of admission that is known, in legal tests for mental incompetence, as "self-incriminating."

But now, suddenly, we're told by some Zodiac observers that the Earth has shifted on its axis, possibly due to epidemic numbers of obese Americans. And this little cosmic jiggle has rifted a rift-shaped rift in the sidereal (but not the tropical) ecliptic coordinates as measured by arc degrees per century along the precession of equinoctial points, resulting in a disambiguation, causing car dealers across America to create Final Disambiguation Sales That Won't Last Long. (Excluding Tags, Title & Rift)

The Zodiac, of course, is that branch of pure science based on the predicate that there are only twelve types of people, a proposition which can quickly be debunked by anyone who's ever been out on a date. I personally know a woman who was seventeen different people, often at the same time. I can distinctly recall one shape-shifting episode involving a hapless waiter who forgot to put the salad dressing on the side. It was downright clinical; it was Lizzie Bordenesque. The waiter may have survived, but after what he went through, I really hope not.

Now, to be fair, there are plenty of other Zodiac types who are calling foul. They say this "new" Zodiac is a load of bunk, which means they think the original Zodiac is *not* a load of bunk, and this is the type of situation that is known, in literary circles, as "a delicious irony."

What is perhaps most fascinating in this ongoing Zodiac versus Zodiac battle is this: according to the Zodiac Redux gang, there's now a whole new star sign, bringing the star sign tally up to thirteen. According to their (ahem) research, the Universe had originally (ahem) created thirteen Zodiac signs, but those meddling Babylonians decided, about 3,000 years ago, at 4:12 on a Thursday afternoon, to just whack one of 'em.

(This is what can happen when you let people run around naming themselves Nebuchadnezzar without insisting on an immediate psychiatric intervention.)

This restored star sign is called Ophuchicus, or possibly Ophuichus. (No, I'm *not* sure. Lighten up. I mean, it *has* been 3,000 years, as of last Thursday, now *hasn't* it? I don't remember what *shirt* I wore yesterday.)

Just as with the correct spelling of the new star sign's name, the Internet is similarly unhelpful on the proper pronunciation of Ophuichus. O-fook-something, O-fuh-something, something-Cuss. But be careful. Mispronouncing a word like that in public could prove rather embarrassing. I remember once being at the cookie counter in a popular hamburger joint, and I badly mangled asking the clerk for a Mother Fuddrucker's Fudge package.

I nearly got arrested.

And you can find almost as many legends about how Ophuichus got nominated to the Zodiac star chamber in the first place. One is the tale of a human named Tiresias (born in darkest antiquity, at 4:12 on a Thursday).

Tiresias, as the legend goes, was a very wise man. One Thursday afternoon, while walking through the woods, he saw two snakes mating, and because this paragraph is not about the legend of *my* life, he did *not* run away screaming. Instead, all very-wise-manliness notwithstanding, Tiresias poked at the snakes (see "bone stupid").

And in that wacky way that things often happened in darkest antiquity, this silly snake-shoving nonsense got Tiresias turned into a woman, assumedly a very wise woman who would know to leave naked snakes alone. Life went on for Tiresias, but with different tax deductions.

Years later, back in the woods again, the (former) guy poked at two more mating snakes, because that's what guys do, even if they're not. And, of course, she got turned back into a man, which is exactly what she deserved to get, after poking at innocent reptiles while they're doing the Humpty Dance.

But the Universe wasn't through with Tiresias yet. Later that Thursday, he somehow managed to irritate Zeus' wife, Hera the Olympian (of the Charleston Olympians), possibly over a sloppily-dolloped salad dressing. Hera got furious with him and, in her trademark, short-tempered immortal way, took away his eyesight and left a really small tip.

Somehow, all this angst caused the Universe to change the poor mortal's name to Ophiuchus (literal translation: "Phudrucker"). And finally, on top of everything else he or she had been through, he got shoved up into the sky to wrestle with a giant python for all eternity. At last, that fateful Thursday was over for Ophie, and this is where we get the expression, "TGIF."

Anyway, before you start running out to Big Slade's Body Art And Hepatitis Clinic to remove your "I'm A Sagittarius So Don't Tread On Me" tattoo (boy, is *that* gonna leave a mark), you should get some qualified Zodiac advice from a qualified Zodiac advisor (keep in mind that they won't *all* be named Tawny or Holar). And don't worry: they're everywhere. According to calculations performed by astronomer and astrophysicist Carl Sagan, there are billions and billions of Internet websites dedicated to bilking you out of a few star-bucks.

And no, this is *not* a plug for Tawny's website. As far as I know, we've never dated.

I do wonder, though, if I ever dated Tiresias. I mean ... you know ... in-between snake prods.

Abby Redux V

(Our angry advice columnist counsels on the current economy)

Dear Abby Redux,
After over twenty years at it, I'm tired of my career as a software developer. Sure, the money's okay, and there's lots of instant gratification, but it's a ruthlessly thankless gig. Over two decades now, and not once has a person ever emailed me to say anything like, "Nice optimized graphics!" or "Thanks so much for the handy navigation menu!" or "Man! That submit button ROCKS!"
So, maybe it's time I moved on. Wonder what else I would be good at?
Signed,
Haven't Dated Since Windows XP

Dear Likely To Snap During A Meeting,
Shut up. I recommend you try working the Returns counter at a Men's Big-And-Tall retail clothing store. I dare you. If you start Monday, you won't last till noon Tuesday. After about eighteen episodes involving some bedroom-slipper-wearing, four-sandwich-eating former beautician trying to get a refund on a six-

pack of Size Fifty-Four boxers with odd green stains on the elastic, that she bought for her still-living-at-home son's 38th birthday, you'll flee – absolutely FLEE back to your solitary sanctuary.

~-~-~-~-~-~

Dear Abby Redux,
I heard on the news that some guy who's being charged for murder is claiming a "caffeine insanity" defense. Is that really a legal option?
Signed,
Bitter In Biloxi

Dear Obviously Not Employed,
Sounds like a red herring to me. Coffee, eh? Why doesn't he just say he's innocent, and lob the blame bomb onto some nearby fast food joint? Where was McDonald's on the night in McQuestion? Eh? Has anybody McChecked the drive-thru clerk's McAlibi? Eh? Where's Perry McMason?

~-~-~-~-~-~

Dear Abby Redux,
While waiting there in the Wals-mart checkout, I done read that some biotechnicalated company has done managed to generically alterize salmons, so them fish'll grow twicet as fast. And them federals say they's gone be safe to eat on. Reckon they safe?
Signed,
Tenured English Teacher In Twin Falls

Dear Likely Purchaser Of Commemorative Railroad Plates,
Which government? The *US federal government*? The government that, after the planet-disrupting BP Gulf disaster, was guaranteeing us that seafood was safe to eat because they had hired professional people to ... ready? ... smell it?
Oh, and here's an idea. Call your elected officials and ask them this: "Twice as fast? Twice as fast as WHAT?" And then please write me back to let me know how that call worked out.
Please.

~-~-~-~-~-~

Dear Abby Redux,
I hate my job. Every day, I work with a person who would have to call in a consultant if you challenged her to spell "dad" backwards. Today, this hair-bearing proto-mammal got all worked up over nothing, and then fired off a semi-literate email, claiming that some persistent customer was "waiting on an answer ASAP."
How do you wait as soon as possible?
Moron. Every bloody day. I hate this.
Signed,
Career Cul-De-Sac In Calabash

Dear Bound To Have A Single-Line Obituary,
Shut up. I can't help you with your particular idiots – I have my own. Morons are like snowflakes: no two are alike, they make your face hurt, and though they always go away eventually, you can't ever figure out when. But I do have some good advice: be nice to that idiot, and smile as long as you're able. Anyone that incompetent is bound to be your boss one day. Count on it.

~-~-~-~-~-~

Dear Abby Redux,
While browsing through a garden catalog, I saw a caption describing a certain plant as a "lovely prostate ground cover." I truly don't mean to be coarse, but surely that's an inaccurate construction, is it not? That's not right, is it?
Signed,
Camellia del Bouquet-Smythe Manigault Perdeaux Ravenel

Dear All That'll Never Fit On The Guest Towels,
I don't know what you mean by "right," but with a name like yours, you cannot *imagine* how tempted I am to blister out a few dozen tasteless "prostate" jokes right about now. Shut up.

~-~-~-~-~-~

Dear Abby Redux,
A conservative running for Congress says she dabbled in witchcraft, but only during high school. Apparently, since then, she's been a model citizen with very few felonious indictments or Faustian agreements. Should we hold that fleeting childhood misjudgment against her?
Signed,
Sarah Palin

Dear Howard Dean,
Are you kidding me? Bring it on. At this point, I don't think one more Washington charlatan is gonna make much difference.
With *this* current crop of career criminals? Please. If they suddenly shape-shifted into winged monkeys during live coverage on CSPAN, nobody would blink an eye. I could sell tickets.
Or maybe not.

~-~-~-~-~-~

Dear Abby Redux,

A West Coast cult took off for a weekend retreat, leaving behind a bag filled with their cell phones and various legal deeds to various pieces of property they owned. The bag caused friends and relatives (and at least one cell phone provider) to fear that the cult members were gonna do something stupid, like commit mass suicide, or change calling plans.

The cult members were finally located and, unfortunately for the local news channel, were completely safe, though they all inexplicably reeked of recently-legalized drugs that once featured prominently in Cheech & Chong movies. They explained to authorities that they had left the bag of stuff behind just in case the world ended over the weekend – just in case "The Rapture" took place before they got back on Monday.

I'm glad they're all okay, but the news raises questions for me. I'm the kind of guy that likes to stay on top of things.

Are you aware of any recently-disclosed theological dogma dealing with specific IRS sub-clauses or real (or administratively non-real) property exemptions specifically targeting non-farm (or off-shore) holdings fully (or partially) claimed (or tangentially discussed) during the fiscal period immediately following the end of the world as we know it, discounting pre-paid sins as subject to the Sistine indulgence allowance (based quarterly) if less than or not less than more than half of the amount on line 22c?

Signed,

Gordon Gekko, Star Of "Wall Street III: Yes, Actually, You Can Take It With You"

Dear Secretary Geithner,
Shut up. You, and the rest of the IRS, just shut up. Get back to running Universal Health Care.

~-~-~-~-~-~

Dear Abby Redux,
I don't want to work at all. But I saw a "help wanted" ad for a copywriter position at a mail-order catalog company. It's an entry-level position, to be sure, and I'll initially be paid a dollar per line of copy. At that rate, I'll be homeless or dead within seven months, but it's honest work and I can see a future for me, and the two illegal immigrant women I live with, and our eleven kids who are all under the age of three. What do you think I should do?
Signed,
Digging Me Some Hope And Change In The New Amerika

Dear Member Of The Final Generation,
I think you should take the plunge! If you still feel that, in the new Amerika, you must work, then do it! You're wrong, but go for it.
But I do have to ask you - not because I care, but because there will eventually be a humor column named "Abby Redux VI" - have you ever had a prostate exam?

Please write me back with your answer.

Please.

Pick a Number

(If you traded in an Infinity, could you prove it mathematically?)

Know how to make a quick enemy? Of course you do. Just start a Facebook discussion about politics or religion. In no time at all, you'll quickly meet all manner of people who share these collective characteristics:

1. They hate you. (they haven't actually *met* you, but that's beside the point)
2. They think you're insane, or stupid, or both. (see Characteristic 1.)
3. But they think they're not.
4. They need just one more "Urky The Pig" Level Three Methane Gas Credit to take over Farmville, a community which doesn't really exist. And they're very excited about it. (see Characteristic 3.)
5. They have the spelling skills of an oyster, but not the attention span.

But sometimes, irritating the general public's just not enough. How do you instantly offend smart people? Easy.

Meet my new friend: Math.

Now don't get me wrong. If I concentrate, and nobody shines a sudden light in my eyes, I can manage to *spell* "math." That's about it. For me to count to six, I have to put down the phone. I have zero math skills. If it's allowed, I have *less* than zero math skills. (I don't know if less than zero is allowed, because I have zero math skills.)

Actually, my Facebook transgression was a trifecta: politics, religion AND math. (see Characteristic 2.) Leave it to me, eh? Anyway, here's the story.

I had been following a debate about proof of Intelligent Design in the Universe (the obvious argument against, of course, being the existence of Congress). One guy made a novel argument in his effort to discount the presence of an Intelligent Designer: the number *pi*, he claimed, was stupid. If this self-proclaimed Math Genius had designed the Universe, he would have made *pi* equal to three, *exactly* three, not some "stupid" endless, three-point-one-four-and-on-and-on-to-infinity fraction.

So now *pi* is stupid. *Pi* just can't get a break. Even way back when I was a kid, which was before the Arabs invented zero, people were making *pi* jokes, jokes like "Hey! Whaddya mean, *pi* are square? *Pi* aren't square -- *pi* are round!"

I didn't say the jokes were *funny*. I just said we *had* some.

And in the ongoing Facebook discussion, that's where I went wrong. I brought up math, which would be like Barney Frank holding forth on ethics, or Barbara Boxer exploring emotional vulnerability. I stated that it was a bit of a leap to jump from *pi* being "sloppy" to God being dead. That's irrational.

Oops.

Suddenly, smart people were barking at me about *pi*, polynomials, irrational numbers, imaginary integers, and something called Euler's number. Somebody immediately barked back: who cares about Euler's number?

Well, Euler, for one. And, probably, his mom.

Personally, I'd never heard of the thing. But you should know that there's an entire "Euler's number" subculture out there on the Internet, packed with the sort of people you probably wouldn't pick for your coed beach volleyball team. In this alternate Universe, you'll discover handy facts like this: In number theory, the Euler numbers are a sequence E*n* of integers defined by the following Taylor series expansion where cosh *t* is the hyperbolic cosine.

As if we didn't already know *that.* Please. That's like the little answering machine voice reminding me that, after I leave my phone message, I can hang up.

And there's lots of "Euler's number" humor out there, too, such as the Letterman-like "Top 1n(e^10) reasons why e is better than *pi.*" Oh, you're killing me! Stop, please. Mercy! Oh, I need oxygen! I also found a helpful Asymptotic approximation, addressing quite large indices obviously based on the displayed lower bound, should you need one during your next tailgate event, or psychotic episode.

I have to point out that, concerning all things Euler, there's a helpful "Ross Tang" online reference, too. I have no clue what that is, but if you think I'm gonna miss an opportunity to say "Ross Tang" then you're not intimately familiar with my asymptotic oeuvre, are you?

By the way: at one of these "We're All Math Geniuses" websites, the wizards have employed one of those "you are visitor number xxx" toys. The simplest of tools, managing math that even I can handle. Take a number. Add 1 to it. Go to lunch.

It was broken.

But then, back at Facebook, the abuse got ramped up a notch. I was now being bombarded by math purists:

- "*ALL* integers are rational, you troll."
- "No bridge on Earth could be built without *pi*."
- "Just wait till I publish my paper discounting the Taylor series expansion. *Then* we'll see what's what, won't we?"
- "If *pi*=3, then all integers would have to be irrational. And guess what *THAT* would do to nuclear warfare! HA HA HA HA HA!"

Speaking of irrational: I'm told that, once upon a time, the state of Minnesota actually passed a law, mandating that *pi* = 3.14, exactly. They legislated mathematics. Now that's ego, folks. I mean, I have an ego you could park a *bus* on. But it's not *THAT* big. That's just, well, irrational.

I still don't understand what an irrational number is, unless we're talking about our national debt. There are irrational numbers, but no irrational integers. Why not? Integers and fractions are rational. Square roots, *pi*, and Euler's "e" are irrational. The movie "Ferris *(b^)*Euler's Day Off" was rational, but only for a while. Something changed. It turned irrational.

What makes a number go irrational? Is there a tipping point? 3.14 bad days in a row, maybe? Is there a domain of insane integers? Psychotic numbers?

Are there co-dependent integers? Integers who are crying out for help? Non-rational numbers that have come to terms with their issues, and voluntarily submitted to a Base-Twelve-Step Program?

At this point, back at Facebook, one of the smart people made another joke: Hey! If we make *pi*=3, then *all* integers will need to be irrational! Whoo!

One day, I have to find and attend a Math Genius convention. It would be worth the effort just to listen in as they discuss the irrational number theory underlying the waitress' tip.

Can't you just hear these smart people as stand-up comics?

"So, a binary set of nuns walked past a bar."

"Subtract my wife. Please!"

"Thanks, ladies and strands of generally-beneficial bacteria! I'll be readily accessible for a full complement of weekdays. Appropriate the veal!"

National Weekday Month

(The new thirteen-page Zodiac-adjusted calendar! Now with Octemberary!)

Universe Experts are trying to convince us that, after a short 23,000-year snooze, the Zodiac moved.

Maybe the Zodiac had a bad dream, or got a leg spasm. Or maybe these experts got a severe head injury after getting kicked by a Zodiac leg spasm.

My guess is that these people sell Zodiac memorabilia, and are trying to recover from a slump. So I've thought of a way for you and me to make some money. A way to get in on this spike in astrology action.

Since the sky's shifted, I'm guessing it's high time somebody created an updated companion calendar. Remember, there are now thirteen star signs! So I'll get to work on a new thirteen-month calendar, and you go round up one more underage nubile bikini-clad Female-Curve-Exhibit dysfunctionally posed on a motorcycle, or a tanned half-naked fireman.

Right now, you might be thinking, "Hey! Who died and made YOU Calendar King?" Or you might not. You might be thinking about firemen, or Curve Exhibits. But, in any case, let's review how we got stuck with our *current* calendar. For our intellectual journey, we'll turn to the Internet. (That last sentence, of course, is its own joke.)

The first Julian calendar was chiseled in 45 BC (literal translation: "Before X-mas"). But other people, who also sell calendars, refer to that same year as 709 AUC ("Anno Urbis Conditae"), while still others think the year was 753 AUC ("A lot of Useless Calendars").

These calendar squabbles, carbon-dating games and price wars went on for Cs of years, until the Dollar Store was invented in the year 537 AUD ("All Under a Dollar"). For the first time, calendars were made available to the general public, so now even regular folk could be late for stuff, too.

And all went well for about IV minutes, until an outbreak of Emperor Justinian resulted in a decree to correct a Late Antiquity (literal translation: "Daylight Savings Time"), which ultimately didn't matter much, given that the bubonic plague outbreaked around 540 AD ("A lot of Doom").

But something was still off. Earlier, in 248 AD ("Attention Deficit"), Philip the Arab (apparently, in the year 248, there was just the one Arab) had celebrated the First Millennium of Rome, together with Ludi saeculares (literal translation: "ludicrous Super Bowl ticket prices") for Rome's alleged tenth 110 years. And it was just this kind of meaningless, mind-numbing tripe that made people call it the "Dark Ages."

Then, in 1582 AD, Pope Gregory XIII took the advice of Aloysius Lilius, a doctor from Naples, and finally scheduled a colonoscopy. (I made that up. Gregory postponed the exam for another XXI anni.) But based on Dr. Al's advice, Gregory changed everybody's calendar, and made it official by releasing a papal bull. Once released, the bull migrated to Pamplona, Spain, where it met Ernest Hemingway. (I made that up. They actually met in Key West.) Pope Gregory XIII finally succumbed to an entirely preventable colon disorder. He was survived by Pope Super Bowl XIV.

The Gregorian calendar is still in use today, at least until we outbreak our new thirteen-month calendar. (I'm still looking for an affordable papal bull.) The Gregorian calendar established a more stable Leap Year Day. Leap Year Day is also known as a Bissextile Day. And bissextile is one of those words you just have to stare at for a few minutes, to make sure you're not missing anything, especially if you're extremely immature.

Admittedly, our current calendar could use a little work. For example, January was named for Janus, an ancient Sabine "dancer" who thought she was AD ("All Dat"). As we now know, thanks to carbon-double-dating, her name was actually Janice, but she lived in the Pre-Dark Ages, in an era before ice had been invented. Some say that Janice was not a woman that I once dated, but was, in fact, a two-faced self-proclaimed deity, and I see no conflict between their story and mine.

And according to the Internet, our current calendar is virtually littered with odd holidays, too.

Each new year, our calendar cleverly kicks off with ... New Year's Day. What a sad commentary on the state of marketing departments during the Dark Ages! Maybe they were just a little off their best game, what with the bubonic plaque outbreaking all over the place. Maybe they were still a bit blurry, due to having invented New Year's Eve first.

It gets worse. Let's review:

January's list of holidays includes a Feast of Fabulous Wild Men Day and a Humiliation Day. Actually, that kinda makes sense. On the other hand, it's both National Bath Safety Month and, in case you mess *that* up, National Blood Donor Month. There's a National Nothing Day and the more inclusive International Skeptics Day. And we find a Penguin Awareness Day, shoved in there somewhere in-between Wild Men and Humiliation.

For some reason, February has become known as the month for Romance, and it viciously guards that moniker. We have Valentine's Day, of course, but it's also National Weddings Month. On the other hand, there's International Flirting Week and Singles Awareness Day.

Lovely. Single guys get *One. Day*. Thanks a lot.

In March, some people celebrate Saint Patrick, but I don't, because I don't live in Ireland. Saint Patrick got rid of snakes, but he got rid of them in the wrong country. But, for the rest of us, we have a Goddess of Fertility Day, appropriately followed by Proposal Day. In March, we also celebrate Extraterrestrial Abductions Day, when we honor various rural American citizens, who all seem to live in "modular homes" and are all, inexplicably, named Zeke. And March has a Multiple Personality Day, too. Or two. Days. Or two days, too. Oh, shut up! No, ***you*** shut up!

April is National Humor Month, which explains both April Fool's Day and the federal tax code. It's National Welding Month, too, though you almost never see any "Happy Welding!" or "During This Time of Annealing" greeting cards. April also hosts Take A Chance Day (not to be confused with Tax Fraud Indictment Day). April's oddly-named Walk Around Things Day sounds interesting, too. And should you forget to walk around things, there's the handy Plan Your Epitaph Day.

Cinco de Mayo is on the fifth of May, and it means "the fifth of May," and as far as I can tell, it celebrates the fact that it's the fifth of May. (I challenge one story on the Internet, claiming that it's a celebration of sandwich condiments.) May's calendar also celebrates both No Socks Day *and* Lost Sock Memorial Day. And speaking of mayonnaise, May is National Asparagus Month, as well as the "National Month" for eggs, strawberries, salad (but not egg salad), barbecue, hamburgers, and mental health. I don't know how Mental Health got shoehorned in here, in the middle of a bunch of food, and in the middle of the year, but I bet Congress was involved.

And just as everybody stops worrying about mental health, June sneaks up on us with National Accordion Awareness Month. Man, that's cold. That's just wrong.

Interestingly, July has a reputation as being unlucky for weddings. Maybe that's because of July's Nude Recreation Week. On the other hand, it's National Anti-Boredom Month, so...pick a weekend.

August was named for Humiditus, a cruel god who was banished to Southern Olympus, forced to wear flannel in summer, and despised humanity for creating ice. Thus, in August, it's too hot to do anything useful, so we sweat our way through National Eye Exam Month and that perennial crowd-pleaser, Wiggle Your Toes Day. Perhaps not so coincidentally, August is also Admit You're Happy Month which, you'll notice, closely coattails July's infamous "wedding blues."

I didn't realize the scope of the crisis, but September plays host to International Square Dancing Month. Apparently, it's not just an American issue. Apparently, square dancing is an international problem, like the bubonic plague. So warn your children: square dancing respects no borders. It's a gateway drug that could lead to polka, perhaps even to ... disco.

September is also National Chicken Month and Mold Awareness Month. And on a lighter note, come the second of September, we all rally round and do ... um ... well, whatever it is people do ... for National Beheading Day. (Thinking about a theme party? For 2 September, the Internet's recommended "recipe for the day" is carrot cake.)

Halloween wraps up October, but before we can slip out of October, we must celebrate World Egg Day, Moldy Cheese Day and Count Your Buttons Day. October is also the Sarcastic Month, which is blisteringly obvious, given that October is both National Vegetarian Month ***and*** Eat Country Ham Month.

November, according to the Internet, is International Drum Month. But according to the Internet, so is October. Lovely. Two whole months, dedicated to drums.

Single guys? *One. Day.*

And then there's December, a special time when we smile, and we sing, and we gather together with our family and friends in meditative love, thanks and worship, as we celebrate the birth of ... the flashlight. Yes, Virginia, there is a National Flashlight Day.

Yeah, I think this calendar's overdue for an upgrade. And we still have to come up with a whole new month! I'm leaning toward Octemberary.

But I better run it by Janice.

By the way - December's also known as National Bingo Month, and we had better grab it and hang on tight. The way things are going in these post-bubonic times, Bingo may be as close to a religion as we'll get.

Abby Redux VI

(Our favorite grumpy columnist greets the elites)

Dear Abby Redux,
This week, at the hotel where I work, our Chamber of Commerce sponsored a charity auction, where a bunch of perfectly styled people drank heavily for about four hours and waved at each other a lot. During the event, this knockout Australian model walked around the ballroom with each item people could bid on, and the auction attendees practically threw money at her.
Heck, I may try this myself. Can anybody hold an auction?
Signed,
Ramon "Bob" Boca

Dear Bob,
I suppose so, you civic-minded monument, you. But I suggest you work your way up to "charity auction." Dream big, but start small, like petty larceny or stealing lunch money from defenseless school kids.

~-~-~-~-~-~

Dear Abby Redux,
Last night, I attended our annual Chamber of Commerce charity auction. I secured a nice, front-row table among my prominent friends, where I successfully bid on and won some sports memorabilia and a politician. I also managed to snag, at a fabulous discount, a weekend of meditation and holistic gastric management, to be held at Gland's End, my favorite sweat lodge in the Virginia highlands. You simply must try them sometime!
Anyhoo, I just wanted to publicly thank the Chamber! And to those who attended, I hope you enjoyed my mid-evening interpretive karaoke of Leonard Cohen tunes.
Signed,
Charles "Chaz" Port au Lett

Dear Chaz,
Can you buy a hat for that ego, or do you just wrap your head in a parachute?

~-~-~-~-~-~

Dear Abby Redux,
Ever been to a charity auction? I have, this week. To fulfill a requirement for my Public Service merit badge, I volunteered to bus tables at a charity auction that my parents went to. It was pretty weird. I'm still not sure what the grownups were doing. Mostly, the grownups stood around in little groups, pointing at other groups, and sometimes waving. Finally, they all sat down and watched a pretty lady walk around the room, holding stuff up, while this guy on stage yelled. The guy was yelling almost the whole time, really fast, saying stuff like "eighty I got eighty eighty doo-ear ninety eighty somebody say ninety ninety doo-ear eighty-five." And every now and then, somebody would stick their arm

in the air and wave a little magazine. This got the yelling guy pretty excited. Weird.
Signed,
William "Will" Williams

Dear Will,
As you'll learn over time, there's no limit to what grownups will do. Wait till you hear about "sweat lodges."

~-~-~-~-~-~

Dear Abby Redux,
At a charity auction this week, I fell in love about forty-seven times with this Australian woman who was presenting all the auction items. I've always been a sucker for an unapproachable woman who will eventually leave and go far away.
Signed,
Name Withheld

Dear Barry,
Just because you created me, that doesn't give you the right to inject your neuroses right in the middle of my charity auction discussion.

~-~-~-~-~-~

Dear Abby Redux,
I am an Australian woman, visiting America and working an internship with the local Chamber of Congress. Last night, I was involved in a charity auction, where a fight nearly broke out over one of the auction items. The item was a $50 gift certificate for what you call hot dogs (those little cased sausages that, in Australia, we call "mystery bags"). I mean, these show ponies,

ready to spit the dummy over mystery bags? You Americans are nuts!
Signed,
Sheila "Lockjaw" Goolabindi

Dear Lockjaw,
Americans? Nuts? I think not.
For example, I've seen groups of apparently educated adults, all wearing variously-colored robes called a "Snuggie," willing to dance around in front of a camera, grinning like their spinal cords have been fused. And this is their JOB, for which people give them MONEY.
No. Americans aren't nuts. Americans are bat-scrabbling insane.

~-~-~-~-~-~

Dear Abby Redux,
At a charity auction this week, I sat at a table behind a woman wearing enough perfume to disinfect Europe. I mean, the woman's olfactory aura would disable your average militia. What is it with women and their perfume Gatling Guns? And by the way: how can a woman wring a live chicken's neck, clean it, chop it up, dress it and cook it, but still be deathly afraid of a spider?
Signed,
Samuel Twain

Dear, um, Sam,
You're not fooling me, Barry. Get out of my column.

~-~-~-~-~-~

Dear Abby Redux,
Last night, I had an interesting evening. At a local event for charity, I decided to bid on a $50 gift certificate for some hot dogs, as a gag gift. Suddenly, from over by the ballroom door, some underdressed rube from the exurbs outbid me! We yelled at each other for a while, until he turned and bolted off, carrying the prize. Fortunately, I had already bid on and won two hours of free legal fees from a local attorney, so I sued the hotel.
Signed,
Ravenal "Pug" Manigault III

Dear Pug,
Are you kidding me? I got five bucks that says that's not your real name.

~-~-~-~-~-~

Dear Abby Redux,
I attended a charity auction this week, and successfully outbid everyone for a fabulous evening at home: a visit by a local chef, who will personally prepare a home-cooked meal of my choosing, for moi and eight of my dearest friends. May I count on you to be there?
Signed,
Delgado "Biffy" Ponderosa

Dear Biffy,
Oh, drat. That evening, I'm already committed to a full schedule of sharpening pencils. I'll have to pass, but in my place I'll send my new friend Ramon. Can he bring anything? Say, fifty or sixty hot dogs?

~-~-~-~-~-~

Dear Abby Redux,
Last night, I was down to that big motel on the freeway for they Happy Hour. After I got right happy, I figured on headin home, but heard a buncha yellin down the hall. I walked along to this hooty-tooty ballroom, peeked in and saw my neighbor Skeeter's boss-woman. I waved at the big-legged ole thing and some guy started pointin at me an yellin "SOLE!" Next thing I knowed, I done won me fifty dollers worth in hot dogs. I nearly had to tighten up this one feller who thought he had a point to make, but after a time, he shut up. I tell you what! Is this a great country or what? It don't get no beddern at!
Signed,
Elridge "Tiny" Curdstill

Dear Tiny,
Here's a little news flash, Herbert Halitosis. You were supposed to PAY for the hot dogs. That was a charity auction, not a Government Cheese drop.

~-~-~-~-~-~

Dear Abby Redux,
I'm one of several authors who recently attended a local charity auction, where we donated signed copies of our books and ate pounds of free shrimp. Later in the evening, the guests bid on a gift basket containing a copy of each author's book. Apparently, though, the gift basket didn't impress: from a funds-raised perspective, our collective literary efforts ranked somewhere between a dozen free car washes and a live dog.
Signed,
Cole

Dear Cole,
Don't ask how, but I know one of your fellow authors, the one who writes a humor column. Believe me, you're better off with the dog.

~-~-~-~-~-~

Dear Abby Redux,
I attended a charity auction this week, and one of the items auctioned off was a small dog. Is that legal, do you think?
Signed,
Clovis "Muffy" Earmough

Dear Muffy,
Let's just hope the people who won the chef and the home-cooked meal didn't bid on the dog.

~-~-~-~-~-~

Comfortably Dumb

(500 million witnesses, and nobody saw anything?)

According to an unconfirmed report on the Internet, a man was murdered today by his own Facebook account.

If this story proves to be true, it would be the first documented case in Internet history of a website killing somebody, if you don't count John McCain's 2008 Presidential campaign.

Pending notification to his eighty-four Facebook friends ... wait, eighty-five friends ... hold on, eighty-six ... no, wait, eighty-five ... the alleged victim's name has not been released to the general Facebook population, his Twitter followers, or his actual physical family. A visitation will be held in Farmville, for those with any compost credits, and the actual funeral and body disposition will be handled by members of the deceased's Mafia Wars inner circle. According to a secondary administrator of his Fan page, the deceased man appears to have passed on peacefully and is lol.

Details of the crime are still sketchy, and theories as to the exact nature of the attack are running rampant. One theory has it that the man got stuck in a Facebook conversation that was so pointless and inane that his entire limbic system just shut down. (He may have posted a desperate plea for help, only to realize that nobody on Facebook knew what "limbic" meant. Instead, somebody started a thread about how George Bush had ruined the Olympic system.)

Some think the poor guy was mauled by an Unwanted Pet, or was the victim of a horribly pessimistic Fortune Cookie, or was gored by a tainted Poke. Others say the "Enter" key on his keyboard got stuck, and Facebook simply liked him to death.

Celebrity attorney Gloria Galldread, who is representing Facebook's HTML code, scoffs at the attack charges. In a prepared statement that she read at least fourteen-hundred-sixty-five times, she claimed that the man simply suffered from an intense bout of depression, resulting from the recent global Facebook service outage.

"It's an understandable misunderstanding," she mumbled, while picking pieces of an ambulance bumper from her teeth. "During the downtime, many Facebook users were forced to go for hours, literally hours, without vital, life-changing personal updates. Nobody could give or receive a Secret Cocktail. Imagine – people simply had no idea what other people were planning to eat for dinner. To be sure, it was a disaster for human society. But murder? I think not."

Other people, who knew the victim, had a more radical suggestion. They claimed the man had a very, very, very powerful computer, and Facebook finally managed to manifest itself as a live, conscious, breathing entity. They envisioned the whole thing like a scene from a science fiction movie, starring celebrity attorney Gloria Galldread. Facebook became self-aware, and then, like any parasite, such as celebrity attorney Gloria Galldread, Facebook crawled across the room and ate its host.

Now, I don't know if Facebook murdered the guy or not. But I have personally watched Facebook kill an entire weekend. Several times. It's not pretty. I've seen it do it.

However, we shouldn't lightly overlook the effect that a Facebook service outage could have on a Facebook addict. The Land of the Numb has claimed many, many victims, inexplicably drawn to skull-thudding commentary like this:

- You have received a Pet Cocktail.
- You haven't changed your profile photo in, like, a whole long time and stuff. lol
- Last night, we had hot dogs with homemade chili.
- Is there any proof in the fossil record that proves or disproves the existence of Barney?
- Hi lol. I going to pick up Junior from soccer lol. I hope nobody gets thrown off the island while im gone rotf! Or has to leave Dancing with the Stars lol HAA HAA HAA!!! I saw a celebrity at a restaurant lol. Who new they 8 and stuff, just like us? rotf
- Homemade chili yum! We had a pot roast lol.
- Please give me any spare pumpkin credits, so I can celebrate having one more goat in Farmville that may one day become a Made Guy in Mafia Wars.
- I *HEART* pot roast! lol
- You have received a Fortune Cookie Horoscope invitation. Click here to irrevocably destroy your computer and any other computer connected to yours. This message brought

to you by a fourteen-year-old wonder-coder sitting in a damp garage in Absurdistan. Click here to like me.

- Pot roast. That's how we role. lol
- You have received a great big fat wet kiss, and based on our review of your browsing history and some of your comments, you are just the type of moron who will believe that it's possible to experience a romantic relationship over a virtual Internet connection. Sitting here in our favorite Internet café in Absurdistan, we *still* can't believe you clicked that attachment we sent. Oh, ye gods, the things I'm about to do to your bank account.

But Facebook does offer advantages, too. Recently, I got a Facebook friend request from someone with the entirely believable name of "Madgalene Scafe." According to a tease from her hidden profile, Magdalene works at "Co" and attended Louis Bromfield High School in Perrysville, Ohio. I'll quote: It is a part of the Mohican Juvenile Correctional Facility.

(Thanks to Facebook's crack security features, I could actually see less of Magdalene's profile than I could see of Magdalene herself.)

Magdalene seems nice, and is hyper-platonically interested in both men and women. She currently has four Facebook friends, all men who lift weights and apparently don't own a shirt.

Magdalene posted an update that she just got "something pierced" yesterday and provided a link to a video. Sadly, what with it being a workday and all, I was all tied up with being sane and didn't get a chance to review her cinematic skills. And ultimately, I had to turn down Magdalene's friend request. I'll hope she'll recover.

Magdalene did provide potential friends with a rather interpretive self-portrait photo which, based on the odd way she was leaning, had possibly been taken during a "how to take in a hem" Home Ec seminar at Mohican Juvenile.

And if you don't think I sold her picture on eBay, then you don't know much.

So. R.I.P., unknown Facebook victim. And the rest of you: just be careful in the Land of the Numb. It's dangerous out there.

Especially when you get an Unwanted Pet Horoscope Fortune Cookie with a Farmville Automatic Weapon Cocktail Credit.

Abby Redux VII

(An odd Valentine's Day for America's favorite irritated columnist)

Dear Abby Redux,
Dude. Thank goodness for, like, co-workers and stuff! omg! Valentine's Day almost slipped up on me again! I, like, totally forgot, like I do, like, every year and all. LOL! My bad!
Signed,
Just In Time

Dear Just,
Just wondering - what's the opposite of "my bad?" My good? And what did you people, like, use, before we, like, invented, like, "like" and stuff?
And yes, co-workers *are* nice. But in your case, I'd give thanks for nepotism.

~-~-~-~-~-~

Dear Abby Redux,
I saw this TV ad for a steamy little Valentine's Day present called the Hoodie-Footie. I'm thinking of ordering one for my old lady.

And the ad says that she can just unzip the left foot part entirely, so that'll come in handy since that ferret accident. The garment comes in some kind of orgasma hatbox, too. Heck, you can even get your Hoodie-Footie montagrammed with a pet name!
Signed,
Jesse "Tiny" Tompkins

Dear Cary Grant,
Montagrammed, eh? I can just imagine that breakfast table conversation. "Honey, how ya spell *bodacious*?"

~-~-~-~-~-~

Dear Abby Redux,
We just got back from my daughter's Fifth Grade League basketball game, where the League schedulers made some kind of terrible mistake. Our poor Fifth Graders were beset by giants! Those opposing girls were *huge*! All the other team's players must live near a nuclear reactor. Four of them were taller than me. Their center, I'll bet, was Fifth Grade Class President for, oh, eleven-twelve years, and two of 'em surely were voted Most Likely To Sell A Jersey And Go Pro. And I'm pretty sure that, at some point in the distant past, I dated their power forward.
But, I'll have to admit, they were very nice young ladies!
Signed,
Extremely Repressed Suburban Male

Dear Tad The Hardy Pioneer,
I'd be nice, too, if I got my sunlight twenty minutes earlier than everybody else.

~-~-~-~-~-~

Dear Abby Redux,
For the Valentimes Day, I reckoned to get my young 'un, Earline, a nice play-pretty. Our innernet provider's got a free "speed upgrade" going on. You reckon my girl Earline would like some free speed?
Signed,
Big Earl

Dear Big,
I'm guessing that, yes, Earline will know what to do when given a bunch of free speed. Yes. Alternatively, you might consider passing along, to your cherished daughter, your equally treasured lifetime membership to Mensa.
Have you guys ever thought about upgrading to the outernet? Ask your "innernet" provider about that. Please. Ask 'em. And please let me know what they say. Please.

~-~-~-~-~-~

Dear Abby Redux,
Did you hear? President Obama finally quit smoking! What a nice Valentine's Day gift to all of us in America!
Signed,
Adoring Fan Of Such Absolute Perfection In A Man

Dear Former MSNBC News Talent,
Let's not get carried away just yet. True, the First Michelle has apparently alleged that her husband has quit smoking. And if she finally set her jaw and put her foot down, I'll bet he did quit, too. I mean, face it - he's gotta live with her.
Heck, look at us! The rest of the country just stands around out here in the street, and she won't even let us eat a Twinkie.

~-~-~-~-~-~

Dear Abby Redux,
An odd thing, to think how many of the puny American males, right now, are putting their romantic relationships in the hands of a tattooed teddy bear, some PJs in a hatbox, or one of those mutated cabana towels known in America as a Hoodie-Footie. Not such, for me. I am Latin. I am full of the romance.
Signed,
Cabrezio del Chesthair Grande

Dear Get Over Yourself,
Eleventh-hour grocery-store flowers again, eh, Casanova? Forgot again, did you, schmuck?

~-~-~-~-~-~

Dear Abby Redux,
Hey, it's me. The guy that created you. I hope you're still having fun, and I still hope you don't mind my creating you. I had to do it, 'cause you'll say things I can't. People are funny about what's funny. It's fascinating to watch where people place their own sacred cows. To him over here, dogs and guns are funny, but not cats. To her over there, cats and Baptists are funny, but not Catholics or guns. Dubya was fair game, but not Obama. I guess banana peels are still funny ... but not when it's your foot.
Signed,
Straw-Head

Dear Dad,
I couldn't agree more. I think there's only one universal constant: Arnold. Nobody doesn't like Schwarzenegger jokes. He's like the Sara Lee of comedy.

~-~-~-~-~-~

Dear Abby Redux,
Eureka! I've found the perfect Valentine's Day gift for my little hottie. Did you know you can order, over the Internet, a custom teddy bear that reflects "what she does at work?"
Signed,
Top Of The World At Twenty-One

Dear So Much Yet To Learn,
Imagine it. "Honey, how ya spell *petty larceny*?"

~-~-~-~-~-~

Dear Abby Redux,
I wrote y'all earlier on, about a Valentimes Day gift for my young 'un. I have since learnt that our innernet provider's "free speed upgrade" is only $39.99 extra a month. That's a pretty spankin' good deal, don't you reckon?
Signed,
Big Earl

Dear Big Earl,
Keep digging, Einstein. I hear their "deluxe" package is even MORE free.
Keep digging. And if you run out of time, you can always lob a little teddy bear or a Hoodie-Footie at Earline.
That, or a camouflage Snuggie.

~-~-~-~-~-~

How To Awesomefy Your Doppelganger

(If you're time-traveling, can you still be late?)

Once upon a time, if you were shopping for weird stuff, you turned to the newspaper and magazine classifieds. But things have changed. Now, you can buy just about anything on the Internet.

Even yourself.

Back in "the day," classified ads ruled. Somebody, somewhere, was always willing to sell an old couch, or a rifle, or one lone orphaned bookend. Classified ads were educational, as well. That's where many of us learned the valuable lesson underlying alluring advertisements such as, "Learn how not to be gullible! Send $5 cash to…"

There were (and still are) flea markets, too, in case you were in need of a large box of assorted nails, some commemorative railroad plates, or a barely-used set of encyclopedias that was missing the volume "ROO to SWA."

A few years later on, late-night TV inherited the role of odd item shopper's mecca, causing thousands of Americans to perk up, sit up and shop: "You know, Pearline, I think it's about time we owned a kitchen knife that can cut through random pre-formed masonry." But time continued to march, and late-night TV was soon supplemented by dedicated shopping channels, which successfully combined the concepts of instant gratification with insane, out-of-control levels of endless, crushing consumer debt.

And then came email and the Internet. Suddenly, marketers didn't even bother waiting for you to want something. No, they just pushed loud, bold, colorful emails at you, over and over and over, and over and over, until you caved in, collapsed on the carpet in a surrendering fetal ball, and started keying in credit card numbers.

And now, everything is available on the Internet. It's all out there, somewhere. Books. Music. Food. Everything is for sale (shipping & handling not included). Cigars, cars and car parts. Pets or furs, or furniture, or pots. Or pot. Vacuums and vacations and vitamins and vice. Drugs. Booze. Everything's for sale. Brides from Moscow. Members of Congress. (mishandling not included)

So, I thought I'd seen it all. I thought I'd seen everything that could possibly be bought.

I was wrong.

Last week, while searching the Internet for a few vials of tiger blood and some freeze-dried Adonis DNA, I was drawn to an ad that invited me to Awesomefy my life. Me! Awesomefy *my* life! Today!

I have to admitilate - my intriguishness was piquefied. I clicked the ad.

The link tookify me to a website that offered to teach me how to take charge of my own destiny by "Quantum Jumping" (as opposed to taking charge of my own destiny by "clicking the 'Back' button"). Quantum Jumping, said the website, is the process of "jumping" back and forth between billions of parallel dimensions, where there are billions of parallel You's. These You's are your doppelgangers, your cosmic twins, each having taken a different existence-path. They are all you, but each on an alternate trajectory, each with different skills, different stains on their quantum carpet, different CD collections and, with any luck, different credit card numbers that would still belong to you, in a quantum sort of way.

Now, speaking of destiny-management, let's dip into current events for a moment. Like everyone else who has no family, or hobbies (or appointments, dates, restraint, self-respect, or TV remote control), I've been following the news coverage of Charlie Sheen. Here's a famous, successful, talented TV and movie star who, if you believe the tabloids, is about two quantum hops away from doppelganging Caligula during Rush Week at Ba'al University.

To be sure, I'm nobody to be giving *anybody* advice. But maybe, just maybe, Charlie could use a little Q-Jumping. Who knows? He might bump into a version of himself that's more like a young Mickey Rooney, or that Timmy kid from "Lassie." I think it's fair to say that Charlie could do worse than give Quantum Jumping a go; otherwise, he's liable to get himself declared a controlled substance and end up in a little bottle with a child-proof cap.

I don't know about you, Charlie, but I'd be bored stiff if I had to live out the rest of my life on a medicine cabinet shelf in somebody's suburban bathroom.

Anyway, the founder (I'll call him "Bob") of the "How To Quantum Jump" site has a name that sounds like an old Iron Butterfly album, and he's from one of those countries that eschewed democratic principles in lieu of managing massive Customer Service call-in centers.

Bob claims that a person, say, you, who wants to be, say, a writer, can use Quantum Jumping to bounce around alternate universes until they find a parallel version of themselves (a doppelganger) who happens to be a brilliant, successful writer in that universe. Then, I suppose, you just eat that doppelganger's head, click your heels together three times, jump back to your own universe, and start cashing royalty checks and fielding offers from Oprah's Book Club.

According to Bob, over 180,000 customers have made successful Quantum Jumps, where they hooked up with their doppelgangers, spent a little quality time with themselves, ate their own heads, scored some instant career skills, and popped back into our dimension ... after, I'm sure, their pre-jump matriculation checks had cleared.

At his website, Bob displays his stellar qualifications by staring straight ahead a lot and holding out his arms like that left-most singer when The Village People launched into "YMCA." Bob insists that Quantum Jumping is within everyone's grasp, through the cosmic principle of "thought transference" and, of course, the more temporal principle of cash transference.

Obviously, Bob's credentials include much more than simply having a very long name and being able to stare at stuff. (I mean, let's face it. Charlie Sheen's credentials could include staring. Before lunch, anyway.) Prior to making insane claims about alternate universes and head-eating, Bob worked in Silicon Valley, and he once published an important paper, entitled "Meditation vs. Tequila."

Or maybe that was Charlie Sheen.

Should you choose to sign up for one of Bob's seminars, you'll learn that all physical matter is the result of particles vibrating at certain frequencies (a theory known in some academic spheres as "Schrodinger's Jello"). During the next session ... assuming you sprang for the two-day package ... you'll learn that, to change one's current reality, all one needs do is change the frequency of one's thoughts. (This is not to be confused with changing the frequency that one actually *has* thoughts. But I see no reason to drag Congress back into this.)

The website's "mission statement" boasts that the company's goal is to spread enlightened ideas to 500 million people, so that everyone can get "a little more awesome." (Awesomer?) To that goal, the company offers a series of brochures and tracts designed to help you Awsomefy your life, as well as an extended weekend retreat that they call the "AwesomenessFest," which they say with a straight face.

Really.

Alert Shopper's Shopper Alert: Apparently, Bob's budget only covers the first 500 million doses of Awesomicity (doppelgangers not included). And, according to an unsubstantiated rumor, there are only about three dozen doses left, thanks to an ad hoc party hosted by all three Charlie Sheens. So call now!

Who knew? Who knew that, on the world wide web, *you* could buy *you*? As I said, I was wrong. Who knew you could just jump on the Internet, learn how to jump around alternate universes, then jump on about 2,500 of your own quantum twins, chomp down on their heads, jump back home, and end up starring in your own sitcom entitled, say, Two-and-a-Half Thousand Men?

Only in America.

But, as the old saying goes, there's nothing new that ends well in the sun.

Or something like that. However that old saying goes. I never learned much about the Solar System ... when I was a kid, my family was missing volume "ROO to SWA."

STUCK IN A J.O.B. WORKIN 4 D MAN OMG LOL

**** Meet the new Boss, grandson of the old Boss ****

Commuter Science

(Fun-filled facts for following fascinating freeway fauna)

Last Friday, for the first time in eight years, I drove to work. Thinking back to eight years ago, I seem to remember it being an overrated experience.

It still is.

Understand - I didn't choose to be driving to work. For eight years, I've been working from home, which is almost the best gig imaginable. The only thing better than working from home is just staying home, not working at all. But that's a very elusive gig that doesn't really pay well, unless you're retired from Congress, or in the Federal Witness Protection Program, or both, which happens more often than you might think, but not nearly enough.

But the company that had been paying me to work from home discovered that I was doing a good job, and working without need of supervision, and turning out a marketable product that they were successfully selling, and all without health insurance or benefits or accrued holidays or vacation days or retirement plan contributions or perks or tax liabilities or office expenses.

So, of course, they had to let me go.

And there it is. Now, like everybody else, I get to commute.

But there's a way to turn even that daily drudge into a learning experience! As you inch down the endless highway each morning ... and each lunchtime ... and each evening ... week after week, week in and week out, month in and year out, decade after decade after decade, until you're just a numbed, drab-colored puddle of ectoplasm that has no reas...

Sorry, I think I dozed off at the wheel for a moment.

Anyway, there's a way to battle the boredom. It's what we call Driver Spotting. It's just like bird-watching, if birds were insanely self-absorbed and drove around in multi-ton vehicles, talking on cell phones while spilling hash browns and gargling Starbucks.

So let's get started! Here's a short, concise taxonomy of some common Driver organisms.

--~~--~~--~~--~~

The Lane Dancers

Like many superior lifeforms, Lane Dancers are better than you and I. And so, when they want your lane, they take your lane. It's very simple. They're just more important, and there's nothing to be done about it. Move out of their way. Or don't. Prole.

The Mascara-y Monster

Many people use their home bathrooms to get ready for work. Not these ladies. Ever since some Detroit schmuck thought it would be a good idea to install flip-down lights and a mirror, the driver's seat has now become an ad hoc beauty parlor. These pouting, lip-pursing ladies don't care that they seem to be trying to soul-kiss the sun visor. Their only goal is to be photo-op ready, even if the next photo they're in is a police accident report.

The Long March Lean-Left Lane Luge

These extra-spatial commuters want to use the center lane to prepare for a left turn, and that's fine. The problem is, they start wanting it some 116 city blocks before they intend to actually turn. You see a very miniature version of them in your rear-view mirror, looming ever nearer, ever growing closer, closing in on their Eventual Left, and as they barrel forward, may the Heavens protect any fool who thinks they also have a Constitutional right to use the center lane.

Ma & Pa Bell

At first, you're concerned, because you think the driver ahead of you has somehow managed to Super-Glue their hand to the left side of their head. But no ... they're just talking on their cellphone. I don't know what they're saying, or who they're saying it to, or why they have to say it now, or how it can take so long to say it. Personally, my life's not that interesting. Often, I can drive nearly an entire mile without having to call anyone and describe what I'm doing. To be honest, I have a sneaking suspicion that these cellphone people are in sinister league with other drivers - drivers in front of me, behind me, next to me. And they're plotting. They're all staging a coordinated campaign against me. They're planning to hit me with a massive Irritation Bomb. Or turn left.

The Ecclesiastic

Okay, hang on to something. It will come as a shock to many drivers when I point out this discovery. But listen, ye, because I have a really fun surprise for you. (and ye) On the left side of the steering wheel is a stick. Seest thou it? Guesseth what? It's attached to lights! Yea! Next week, we'll talk about what those lights do! Here's a hint: to everything, there is a season. Turn! Turn! Turn!

The Eternal Turner

And then, the week after that, we'll talk about using that neat little stick to turn the lights off! Yes, I'm talking to ye! Because your turn signal has been blinking "left turn" since Hannibal double-parked Dumbo!

The American Dashboard Idol

Almost always a male, these guys. Slapping the steering wheel, pounding the faded polyurethane dash, air-guitaring to the 4-4 beat of some robotic rock tune. It's never rap, or country, or jazz. It's always some tune by some band named Ulcerous Lesion, or Baal's Lunchbox, or Throb, with a lyric like "She walked too heavy and WAAAAAAAAAAAAAAAA!"

The Exurb Troop Transporters

Soccer moms. Mama grizzlies. Over-zealous Catholics. Whatever. Through whatever means, these are distaff errand-monsters who have collected (or given birth to) some sixty-seven dozen chocolate-crazed children, shoehorned the entire invasion force into the family's Suburban Assault Vehicle, and are heading for a take-no-prisoners play date at Skully's Fun Park of Death and Pizza Buffet. From your viewpoint, all you see are bouncing tykes, as if Stephen King had hijacked a school bus, electrified the seats, and Quentin Tarantino had optioned the movie rights.

The U.N. Shuttle

You've seen these vehicles. In some aspects, they're similar to the Exurb Transporters. Standard four- or six-passenger cars, but as you approach them from the rear, you can clearly see at least eleven dozen heads which, for some reason, always seem to be crowned with black hair. No one in the vehicle ever moves a muscle. There's always some vaguely Catholic-looking ornament hanging from the rear-view mirror. The car looks to be worth about twenty bucks, but the cautious commuter never ventures out of the rightmost lane, and never teases the engine above thirty MPH.

Pollyanna Has Left The Building

These are drivers who, due to having been born with an extra optimism gene, seriously think they're going to be allowed to turn left out of a parking lot, across several lanes of commuter traffic. For some reason, these "I'll just quickly turn left here" optimists are usually women. It never crosses their mind to make a RIGHT turn, to go WITH the flow of traffic, and then make a calm, easy left-left U-turn somewhere down the road. And so they will sit there, and sit there, and sit there, until some pitying driver finally motions for them to sneak in front. At that point, Pollyanna has to play the same sneak-pity game for the next oncoming lane, and the next, and so on and so on, until people who've never met her hate her guts.

The Sweet Spot Squatters

At some point in Fairy Tale history, trolls figured out that, if they hung around bridges long enough, they would haul in some serious coin, not to mention body parts. (Later on, the IRS figured out a similar scheme) Our modern-day commuter trolls have learned that, if an intersection is already full of cars, there's no need to patiently wait for the next traffic light cycle. "Better to just shove my vehicle into the intersection, too! Maybe then, when the light changes, I'll be able to completely block traffic in ALL FOUR DIRECTIONS! Whee!"

The Warp Jumpers

These are those drivers who see that yellow traffic light, not as a clue to slow and wait, but rather as some kind of cosmic dare. That amber bulb triggers some kind of kamikaze impulse, causing the driver to punch in the afterburners, and to try and Han Solo their earth-bound vehicle through the intersection, often from several blocks back, before the lights rolls to red. Not surprisingly, this is often explained away as "a guy thing."

The Hand Talkers

For some commuters, a larynx is not enough. They must also communicate with their arms and hands. From your perspective in the car behind them, they seem to be in dire need of an exorcism, or are possibly victims of some rare torso-based Tourette's Disease. Since they must communicate or die, Hand Talkers usually commute in pairs. For some reason, they usually smoke, too, which is an excellent way to get an optional larynx.

Aesop's Truants

Eight miles an hour. In traffic, or in the grocery checkout, or in the all-you-can-eat buffet. Eight miles an hour. In the bank line, in the toll-booth line, in the movie ticket line. Eight miles an hour. At the deli, at the doctor's, at the dime store, at the doom of history. Eight miles an hour. 'Nuff said.

--~~--~~--~~--~~

Well, there you are! Now you're ready. Happy spotting! The next time you head out for your morning commute, grab your binoculars and this handy guide, and enjoy the wildlife on America's highways and byways!

And as you peer at other drivers with your binoculars, be sure to stare and point a lot. If you get the chance, throw some bird seed at their car. You're sure to make lots of friends!

Airport Insecurity

(Fear and loathing for the frequent flyer)

You don't need me to tell you this, but these are tough, dangerous times. There are people trying to kill us, people daring to disregard things we own, people willing to steal things we need.

And that's just at the Wal-Mart pre-Christmas sale.

For some *real* danger, insults and insanity, try flying! It's gotten completely nuts. From the time you leave your house, the whole experience has become a gauntlet. It seems like the goal of everyone you meet is to hurt or rob you, charge or fine you, molest or arrest you.

I was invited to appear at a book signing, in a city about 300 miles away. And because I'm an idiot, I accepted the offer. It wasn't the cost of the flight, mind you: the host agreed to treat for that. What makes me an idiot was thinking I had any chance of selling my little monkey book amid the avalanche of authors releasing new books to bookstores, often by the hour. Stephen King, for example: I'm convinced that the man can be handed a royalty check for his latest bestseller, hop in the car, and then write another book *on the way to the bank.*

LITERATURE UPDATE: George W. Bush's new book, "Decisions I Made And Some I Probably Should've Made But Didn't," sold 750,000 copies in its first week. My last book sold about eight. Maybe I need to rethink my protagonist.

Anyway, due to new TSA security procedures, I had to check in at the airport five months before my flight. So I packed a bag and my copy of Glenn Beck's new book, "How Touching Anything Can Kill You," and hit the highway.

Even the drive to the airport subjected me to serious risk. Freeway traffic got stalled when one of the new "Dolt" sub-compacts from General Tso Motors ran out of electricity. A bit farther along, a committee of IRS agents putting up yet another "This Is Yet Another Shovel-Ready Project Road Sign" road sign stripped a screw and the sign collapsed onto the shoulder, seriously injuring three hitch-hiking, out-of-work non-union laborers.

LITERATURE UPDATE: George W. Bush's new book, "I Didn't Kill Anybody's Wife, But If I Had, Here's How I Would Have Done It," sold 750 million copies in its first week. Celebrity attorney Gloria Allred took out a full-page ad in the L.A. Times, offering to file civil charges on behalf of anybody named "Anybody."

Due to new TSA security procedures, I was not allowed to leave my car idling at the curb outside the airline's check-in, but I did have the opportunity to donate my pocket change to a vacuous smiling woman wearing sandals, a pastel robe, and tapping a tambourine. As I drove off, the grinning panhandler was approaching an oddly-familiar fellow, unshaven and sporting a Super Bowl ring.

HOMELAND SECURITY UPDATE: Following an airport security pat-down, superstar quarterback Brett Favre has allegedly sent "unsolicited" photos of himself to a young, undercover TSA agent named "Bambi," who was involved in the frisking.

Since new TSA security procedures required me to be at the airport several months prior to actually getting on the plane, I drove the half-mile out to long-term parking. But it had been temporarily closed by airport security after an engine fell off a passing Qantas jet and cratered the parking lot, seriously injuring three hitch-hiking, out-of-work small business owners.

LITERATURE UPDATE: George W. Bush's new book, "I Didn't Drive the Economy Into A Ditch, But If I Had, Here's How I Would Have Done It," has just screamed up the best-seller list, leaping past Sarah Palin's new book, "How To Field-Dress A Liberal." In an obvious snub, Oprah announced plans to interview Joe Biden about his new book, "Tourette's Is A Great Big *** Deal."

On the walk back to the airport, I nearly got run over by two UPS couriers who flew past me, hurrying to re-stock the airport gift shop with fresh copies of six new books that Glenn Beck had written since breakfast. Oddly enough, the couriers blew right past airport security.

HOMELAND SECURITY UPDATE: An overseas traveler has tried to blow up Detroit by sneaking onto a plane with an inkjet printer hidden in his underwear, causing Homeland Security to institute new security procedures that outlaw hiding inkjet printers in one's underwear. Superstar quarterback Brett Favre has allegedly sent "unsolicited" photos of himself to the printer's toner cartridge. At a press conference, Joe Biden made the comment that blowing up Detroit would be redundant.

In the airport, I walked past the "Designated Smoking Area," a foul-looking, stale-smelling squared hole in the wall accessible, not by a standard door, but by parting a pair of those large, unwieldy flaps of industrial-weight plastic, the kind you see bolted above the entrance of restaurant meat freezers, or high-radiation-level weaponry labs.

LITERATURE UPDATE: George W. Bush's new book, "I Didn't Launch A Missile Attack On California From A Clandestine Nuclear Silo On Catalina Island, But If I Had, Here's How I Would Have Done It," has been translated into Mandarin, and Quentin Tarantino has picked up the movie option.

Since I had some time to kill, I thought I'd get something to eat at the airport diner, but instead I got detained and questioned for writing a potentially threatening phrase like "some time to kill" in a humor column about airport security.

HOMELAND SECURITY UPDATE: Members of Congress called for hearings, challenging Homeland Security for not doing enough to protect members of Congress who often had to fly to various Caribbean Islands on illegal, taxpayer-funded junkets. The agency responded by instituting new security procedures that outlaw underwear, and shoes. Championing the new security procedures, Brett Favre agreed to volunteer as a TSA agent, calling it his patriotic duty.

Back at the airport, I finally managed to shake off Agent Favre and I purchased a tuna fish sandwich. For twenty-eight dollars. Oh, yeah. That's fair. That's about right. Sheesh. I didn't want to *marry* the sandwich; I just wanted to stare at it for a few minutes.

HOMELAND SECURITY UPDATE: HomeSec Secretary Janet Napolitano has come under fire for the agency's new and extremely unpopular "layered security" measures at the nation's airports (measures which include the controversial and invasive full-body pat-downs) after a review of the new security procedures uncovered this directive:
"Afterwards, you should offer the passenger a cigarette."

LITERATURE UPDATE: George W. Bush's new book, "I Didn't Co-Opt a Printer From A Child Labor Sweatshop In Yemen, Pack It With Explosives, And Shove It In My Underwear, But If I Had, Here's How I Would Have Done It," sold 750 million copies before he wrote it. However, due to new TSA security procedures, he was not allowed to use a printer to print the book. A well-known Washington state software magnate released a digital version of the book, and was then arrested for illegally bundling eReader software with its operating system.

By then, I'd had enough. Forget the book signing, forget the flight, forget the tuna fish sandwich that requires a co-signer. I grabbed my bag and my book and headed for the escalator. Enough.

Unfortunately, due to new TSA security procedures, once you've begun the TSA security process, you can't leave. I'm dead serious: I am not good enough to make this stuff up. Once you've entered the TSA's august zone of authority, you may not leave the airport without submitting to a TSA security interview.

In a blast of bureaucratic genius, they have decided that they're gonna profile people who are *leaving* the airport.

Fortunately, though, I managed to create a diversion and escape. Grabbing an inkjet printer from my left sock (security oversight!), I made an "unsolicited" photo of my tuna fish sandwich and threw it at Brett Favre. This distracted the superstar TSA agent, allowing me to hit him with one of Glenn Beck's new books, "You're All Dead: They Just Haven't Told You Yet," and then I stunt-rolled out the airport's automatic doors to freedom.

HOMELAND SECURITY UPDATE: A couple of weeks ago, I ordered an airline ticket online. Three days later, at about 7pm, a TSA security guard wearing cocktail attire and carrying a bouquet of flowers showed up at my house, flashed a badge, and subjected me to a full-body pat-down.

Oddly, her name was "Bambi," too.

I couldn't complain, now could I? Because if I complain, then the terrorists win.

Things To Not Say At Work

(How to win friends, influence people, and get fired)

Okay. It's been a week now since I started working for somebody else, and nobody's killed anybody. That's promising. In an office environment, zero fatalities is an excellent metric. It's a very good start.

In some ways, moving from one job to another can be compared to Indiana Jones, tentatively tapping his way across a bottomless abyss, one unsteady stone at a time. But it can also be viewed a learning experience, a teachable moment, like teasing a mongoose, or eating too much Mexican food. And the moment's made even more poignant if, up to now, you've been working alone, or working for yourself, or working from home, or all of the above.

Trust me.

Working from home is a wonderful thing, but it's still a very rare thing, like never losing an argument, or military intelligence. There are things about working from home that you know you'll miss. Casual Friday occurring five days a week. Ignoring emails for three days and then blaming it on your ISP. Participating in phone conferences while wearing nothing but socks and a ski mask.

And then there are things you won't realize you miss until they're gone, like naps. Taking off for the coast for four days and billing it as "geopositional research." Claiming ski masks as an itemized deduction.

Here's a free tip. Ever been sitting around at home, and you just spontaneously break out into song? Don't do that at work. For that matter, don't do that anywhere in public, especially if there are mental health professionals around.

Trust me.

So if you find yourself in a situation that requires you to actually leave your house and go work somewhere, you'll want to remember some things as a new employee, in order to maximize your enjoyment and minimize your embarrassment. For example, it's highly likely that there are going to be people around. That, I suppose, is the main thing to remember about working in public.

And, as a new employee, one of the things you'll enjoy is the "new employee" office tour, during which you will get to wind your way along many office hallways, examine many closed office doors, and possibly meet the three people who are actually *at* work that day, though probably not, because they're in a meeting, or at lunch, or "off-site" doing geopositional research.

But if you should chance to actually meet anyone who's on the payroll, watch your mouth. You never know who you're talking to, especially when you're the new guy.

Shortly, we'll offer a helpful quiz, to better prepare you for the intricate interplay that is inter-office communication. But first, and all for your benefit, we've put together a little list of things you should just not ever say at the office. Ever. Period. Just don't. Ever.

Trust me.

--~~--~~--~~--~~

The Little List:

- Who was *that* clown?
- Don't you people ever cuss?
- I haven't laughed that hard since Grandma died.
- Is it just me, or is the President an idiot?
- What's *your* extension? No, wait. Let me guess. 666.
- I never see *you* doin' much work. How much they pay *you*?
- You *work* for that clown?
- What are you, *nuts?* It's nearly 2:30! No way I'm starting anything *new* today.
- That was a fairly stupid email you just sent.
- You don't think anybody'll notice if I pocket a few office supplies, do ya?
- No sweat. If you bend it twice, the time card's unreadable, anyway.
- So, you like "dead cat" jokes?
- Can you imagine anybody *dating* that clown?
- Aw, shoot. I didn't know it was "Wear a Stupid Tie" day!
- Sorry I'm late. I ran over another dog.
- Oh, go get bent! Who do you think you are, the owner's daughter?

--~~--~~--~~--~~

The Helpful Quiz:

While being introduced to a female coworker, you notice framed pictures of children in her office. What is your optimal comment?

1) Who's that? Your grandkids?
2) You know, that's nothing a little orthodonture couldn't fix.
3) Can I use your phone? That kid on the right, I saw on a milk carton.

While being introduced to a male coworker, you notice framed pictures of children in his office. What is your optimal comment?

1) That your daughter? *Man*, she's hot.
2) Nice-lookin' kids. Any idea who the mother is?
3) I'm confused. Bob Roberts in Marketing said you were gay.

As a sales professional, you've been asked to advise on a "delicate" inventory transaction, which may present global implications to the company, both financially and legally. What is your optimal advice?

1) I've hit this month's quota. I don't care if it sells or not.
2) Okay, look heah. Find out what Senator's on the oversight committee. Contact Tito and The Fat Man. Bill it to petty cash. Call the Senator. Use a pay phone. Capiche?
3) Oh, please. What are the chances we'll get audited two years running?

You've just been given a tour of the company's public-facing website. All you could think of was a severe bullet train accident. It looked like the battle of Shiloh. The thing had more typos than Paris Hilton's ninth-grade term paper. What is your optimal analysis?

1) Stop it. Your cousin's nephew did all this, for free? Get out. Really? You could've knocked me over with a feather.
2) I'm not one to quibble, but nobody's used "Ye Olde Presse Release" in quite some time.
3) Love the spinning black-and-purple logo. Got any Velour fonts?

As you're being introduced to a female coworker, you notice that she's ... well ... let's say, dressed comfortably. What's your optimal convivial observation?

1) So when you due, Freida Fertility?
2) Whoa! Bob Roberts in Marketing was right! I bet you'd bring an all-you-can-eat buffet to its knees, eh?
3) Are you the *entire* group insurance policy?

During your initial meeting with the company's Board Chairman, it quickly becomes apparent that Captain Nepotism here is about two genes shy of having webbed feet ... eventually. What is your optimal greeting?

1) I'm very much looking forward to working here, sir. Can I get you anything? Drool bib? A "Flintstones" lexicon? Krill?
2) That's a bold choice, sir. Not everyone will eat the colored chalk.
3) I love your nails, and I want to have your children. Sign this.

--~~--~~--~~--~~

Well, I hope this little primer helps prep you for a good start in the corporate environment. I'm sure you'll fit right in! Be smart. Be subtle. Retain all your receipts. Keep moderately clean. And remember ... when all else fails ... be honest. Honesty is the best policy, and the most certain key to your success.

Because once you can fake honesty, you're home free.

Trust me.

He Said WHAT?

(We should always honor perfection. Even when it's stupid.)

I love lists. Ever since I saw the first back cover of my first album, I've loved lists. Lists let me know what to expect, and when to expect it. Lists let me know if there's more stuff, what stuff comes next, when stuff is over. All of life should be that easy.

So here's a list for you, one that addresses that age-old question: "so just how stupid *is* he?" It's not presented in any particular preference or order. As far as I know, I made up the whole list, often right in the middle of reading an email, so feel free to lift any item in my list, for any purpose you find appropriate. You never know. As a wonderfully wise woman once told me, "don't ever let stupid people get you down, 'cause you're never gonna meet the last one."

Maybe, one day, you'll need to make a joke, or close a deal, or seal a job interview. Or maybe you'll just simply feel a sudden need to seem superior to people you're not, in fact, superior to.

(Take, for example, those yawn-dart purists who would like to stab you in the neck for ending a sentence with "superior to.")

This is a list that has value in any place or time. It could seem even more relevant right now, given our proximity to a Congressional election season, but that's just one of life's delicious coincidences, like $90,000 turning up in the freezer of Louisiana Democrat William Jefferson ("I have *WHAT?*"), or Sarah Palin suddenly appearing in Iowa while adamantly considering not theoretically running for President. ("I'm where?")

For expediency's sake, I'll use the male pronoun throughout the list; however, the list applies equally to males and females, or however many genders America has this week.

Besides, I don't need any more women mad at me. Women already treat me like some kind of half-clothed freak because I hold doors open for them, an action which used to be a sign of common courtesy but, at some point in recent American history, appears to have become an infuriating chauvinistic insult. I must've missed that meeting, probably while I was out insulting waitresses by leaving them tips and complimenting their smiles.

So. Without further ado, let's discuss "stupid." Enjoy!

- He's so stupid that I sometimes wonder if he's twins. No one human being could be that stupid.
- He's so stupid that he wore a tie to work because he heard that a customer was "receiving miss information."
- It's the kind of stupidity that blots out sunlight.

- He's so stupid that I worry about his neck. The slightest breeze, and that unoccupied skull could collapse like a Mylar balloon.
- He walked disappointedly out of the lunch buffet, because the Sneeze Guard sign read, "Please use a new plate for each visit," and he hadn't thought to bring any new plates with him.
- He's so stupid that I don't how he manages to dress himself without poking out an eye. And I mean the eye of a human in the car in the lane next to him.
- He says stuff that's so stupid, I question *myself.* I worry that I'm hallucinating, because no mammal with a larynx would say anything that stupid.
- He's so stupid that I drove three hours to his office, just to see what he *looked like.* I had to know. I wanted to see if it *showed.*
- This is ... I don't *know* what it is ... stupid cubed, maybe. It's staggering. I don't think I'm being fully appreciative of the spectacle I'm witnessing. It's a gift. I'm in awe. I should sell tickets.
- I don't know where his retinas are sending their information.
- He's so stupid that he publishes a "How To Be Stupid" newsletter. (Actually, he does no such thing, but he's so stupid that I told him he *was* publishing a newsletter, and then talked him into writing me a check for the postage to mail his newsletter.)
- He says stuff like, "I need you to undo what you did when we did that thing so we wouldn't have to undo what he did after we were. O?" For all I know, that's an encrypted military code from the Vatican, okaying the carpet-bombing of Baptist hot-dish suppers in Cleveland.

- He's so stupid that he bought a car because it featured "air, power steering and way more," and the car salesman managed to talk him into buying an optional leather case for his "way more."
- It's a very special cerebral structure that allows an even moderately-endowed biped to think up questions like, "If I change the file, will that make it different?"
- Again. He forgot again. He forgot *AGAIN*. I don't know how he remembers, two days in a row, to wake up.
- I need a ruling. This one ... this person is ... you weren't there, so you can't ... this is ... this one may need to be ... how do I put this gracefully ... did you ever see the movie "Old Yeller?"
- He's stupid as if stupid were a gift from Zeus.
- Not his fault, of course. It goes without saying that this level of damage is the result of some violent childhood playground accident, possibly involving sharp objects and an unsupervised vise, or prank-pulling thugs from some disgruntled Teachers' Union, or water fountain contamination from a nearby nuclear spill.

So there you are. Hope that helps, one day, when the time and place call for it. Cause they're out there, ready to amaze you. As someone much more clever than I likes to say, "Did you hear that? Whoa. He may not be smart, but he sure is stupid."

You may be wondering if this list is a "tribute" to a specific person. If my compilation could have been triggered by some recent staggeringly stupid event.

And if you come back in an hour, or a week, or a month, trust me - you'll still be wondering.

After all, I mean ... c'mon. I'm not *stupid.*

Dear Santa: Send Lawyers, Guns & Money

(Christmas Presents For Guys! As Lied About On TV!)

Well, it's that time of year again: that magical season when we celebrate the birth of someone whose name, apparently, is "Holiday."

But that's not really important. The magic of Christmas is in finding a gift that's at least a buck more expensive than that bobo gift your co-worker got you last year.

And as a public service, our staff is here to help, even though, like public service, our staff doesn't actually exist!

So without further ado, our staff (shut up) presents our (my) reviews of this year's hottest holiday gift ideas!

- For the reader: Barbara Bush's "Why Sarah Palin Had To Leave Idaho"
- The Enough Already Corporation introduces a TIVO-like TV recorder that will zoom past bone-care ads where Sally Field obsesses about having to choke down a whole pill

every day. This invention may, in our avuncular opinion, deserve a Nobel Prize.

- Sadly (but not surprisingly), the Snuggie is back, and back with a vengeance. The Snuggie, of course, is that androgynous A-line couch-wear that, when donned in private, turns the wearer into a grinning idiot, like Jack Nicholson in the *good* Batman movie. It gets worse. Occasionally, an entire group of Snuggie-cloaked people will appear in public, in the same place and at the same time, all mathematical probabilities notwithstanding. If any unwitting eyewitness manages to survive all the Snug-induced grinning, they'll likely not survive the orgiastic group dancing that follows. (Note: Snuggie devotees tend to frequent sports events involving young children, and during this festive season, I should move away from that joke right this minute.)
- For the reader: Rahm Emanuel's "A Sale of Two Cities"
- Debuting this year in the Christmas gift category is medical supplier Rear Echelon Orthotics, who offer a handy workplace device that will analyze whether someone in the office cafeteria is offering you additional dietary fiber for some weird, self-serving purpose, or simply because they really like you. (avuncular non-threatening Indian spokesman not included)
- Tech giant Huge Lit Packers has a new remote-access device that seems to work like this: when you press a button, a large chunk of land detaches itself from the mainland, travels through the tropics, dashes through the Arctic, snakes its way up an urban river channel, slides through a business district, and slams into an office building, causing a color document to get printed. (Inside the office building, no one

notices when a foreign land mass crashes into their midtown superstructure. Maybe it's the offices of the FAA.)

- For the reader: Glenn Beck's "A Book of Stuff I Thought Up Since Last Week's Book"
- The makers of CLR, everyone's favorite household miracle cleaner, present CPR! CPR: a fast-acting powerful neurotoxin: simply drink one cup of CPR and never worry about cleaning again! Now in lemon-lime! (Last Will & Testament not included. Last rites and avuncular priest sold separately.)
- For the reader: "Jane Eyre Gets Regular" (Rochester discovers that his bitter, arson-leaning wife had gout. Plus, she's dead, which knocks down several "Wonder if Jane's busy?" bowling pins. He agrees to marry Jane, but only if she will begin a regimen of Bifidus Regularis and Sally Field-endorsed pro-biotics.)
- The popular board game "Where's Waldo?" gets a new treatment with "Where's Wadi?" Hilarity ensues as politically-hamstrung UN inspectors try to locate arms dealers before the (included) Mayan Calendar timer goes "Boom!" Fun for the whole family! And the "Where's Wadi" Bonus Round is sure to be a hit at frat house New Year's Eve parties! Simply attach the two exposed wire leads (included) to any standard car battery, start the Mayan timer, and hunt, hunt, hunt! But hurry! (Battery not included. If the timer expires, some reassembly may be required.)

So, happy shopping! And may I mention that I need a new putter, I love power tools, and I'm unimaginably shallow, self-centered and stupid!

Just like every other male in television ads!

Three Mittens For Tim's Cat

(Toothpaste, toys, tires and TVs? In the same shopping cart?)

Here's a little free tip: never shop for high-end electronics in a retail store that's advertising deep discounts on tube socks.

It wasn't entirely my fault. It was a weekend, I had an urge, and nobody was around to slap me out of it.

I was on my own. Nobody snorted and scoffed, "You can't be serious." I had no alert spouse ... no on-duty, en garde guardian angel ... no little Jiminy Cricket to bitterly tap his little cricket umbrella, shake his little cricket head, and chirp, "*Where*, pudding-head? You're gonna buy what, from *where?*"

Let's be honest. One of the downsides of being a single guy is that no one is standing by to monitor your impulsive behavior. I don't know for a fact who coined the expression, "seemed like a good idea at the time," but I bet it was a single guy, and I bet he ultimately got to that rueful state because nobody was around to kick him back inside the house.

Understand - it's not intentional, premeditated stupidity. Single guys have a conscience, mind you. We just don't have much of a memory. I suppose it's some kind of pudding-head recidivism.

Stupid done is stupid forgotten.

So, anyway, here's how I managed to mess up (*this* week).

It was the mid-morn of a lovely, cloudless Saturday, when I felt it begin to wash over me ... all the symptoms of an unfulfilled "new toy" binge (single guys reading this will completely understand). I had even fixated on the exact toy - an expensive pair of top-shelf stereo speakers, so that I could install them at my office at work, so that I could immediately begin not listening to them, since there are other-people-in-the-room-thank-you-very-much, and they're trying-to-get-some-work-done-if-you-don't-mind, and besides, they don't see how anyone past the age of Early Fetus can stand listening to Hall & Oates anymore, but here's a rushed, low-quality MP3 of my third cousin's brother's grunge-inspired garage band, named Furious Blistered Lesion, that has a gritty ensemble feel that reminds me of what drug-crazed ferrets must sound like if caught in a hay baler, don't you think?

But it's Saturday. Let's not drag work into this.

Because it was too early for the "real" stereo stores to be open (and because I wanted the speakers right now, rather than, say, thirty minutes from now), I eschewed patience and headed out for a quick point-and-pay episode at that shopping mecca, that We-Never-Close wonder known as Uber-Mart. ("Eschew" is an Olde English word that means "Patient? Later, I'll be patient.")

As you no doubt know, if you live on or near Earth, an Uber-Mart is a massive, invasive structure, built at monstrous expense, often requiring the store to purchase its own traffic lights, zoning variances, Papal indulgences, and Congressmen. I'm told that in America's heartland, in places like Wisconsin (which is near Earth), there are several Uber-Marts that have their own zip code.

I drove to the nearest Uber-Mart, some seventy yards from my house, which took me past twenty-seven McWendy Kings, 114 Baptist churches and fifty-eight pharmacies. Welcome to the deep South.

Granted, having to drive seventy whole yards just to get to an Uber-Mart is a bit cruel, but there it is. We do what we must. Still and yet, it's a cold, cruel world. Witness: from the Uber-Mart closest to me to the next nearest one demands a drive of over eighty-five yards ... and to get an Uber-Mart beyond *that* one, you'll have to drive nearly *eight entire city blocks*, if you can imagine such an inconvenience. And this should give you some idea of how downright Spartan things can sometimes get, here in the deep South. ("Spartan" is an Olde English word that means "Honey, we got any clean tube socks?")

The layout for an Uber-Mart is always the same: the store lurks behind a parking lot the size of a minor galaxy, or Paul McCartney's alimony payment. The twelve-umpty-acre building generally presents its patrons with two time-saving entrances, often situated in the same time zone. One entrance is for eyeglasses and groceries, and the other for gardening supplies and tube socks (plus a smaller door for "boutique" services, like dental implants, pet funerals, and exorcism catering). For some unexplained reason, about a quarter of the parking lot's prime real estate is never available for any actual parking, but always seems to be reserved for bags of peat, paving stones and fence parts.

And the fun has only begun. Nothing as ferociously vast as an Uber-Mart can exist without some level of complication. See, despite the tundra of parking and the gaping doors, it's not possible to actually get inside an Uber-Mart without first running the Charity Gauntlet. Standing between you and the Uber-Mart's alluring, air-conditioned interior, there is inevitably some emaciated waif, with eyes the size of Druid crop circles, ringing a tinny bell and hoping to guilt you into dropping a few coins in her dented, discolored collection bucket that bears a Dickensian hand-written plea like "Please help save Timmy's kitty's left leg."

The other door will be guarded by a hyperactive group of twittering juveniles selling limp chocolate bars, or raffling chances to win a double-aught squirrel rifle, so that the East Grizzle Junior High School Marching Band (the "Hayloft Mites") will have enough money to attend this summer's annual Beans-N-BBQ Jamboree and Prophylactic De-Worming at the State Capitol.

And each entrance-guarding garrison of youthful entrepreneurs will be flanked by a questionable-looking collection of middle-aged, scale-tipping diabetes candidates in lawn chairs and discount tube socks, hawking tepid hot dogs in damp, red-tinted buns.

And on this Saturday, sadly, I slipped up while running the gauntlet. I made eye contact with The Guardians, which left me with no elegant options. No graceful escape route. So I bought a hot dog, gave it to Tiny Tim's sister, pitched in to help save the cat and, I'm fairly sure, co-sponsored a Sousaphone.

Once inside, I focused, laser-like, on my original mission. I navigated to the Electronics section at the very back of the Uber-Mart complex, arriving just as the weather cooled and the leaves began to turn. I scanned the shelves and quickly grabbed a suitable set of speakers. Oh, and a jacket to ward off the Autumn chill.

Done!

And lo, less than three hours later, I hauled my six bulging shopping carts into the "Self-Checkout" zone. ("Self-Checkout" is an Olde English word that means "Okay, I tried patience, and didn't much care for it.")

Almost done! Swiped my credit card, bagged my jacket and my new set of speakers. And a rake. A box of U.S. President pencils and a flagon of hot mustard. A deluxe "50th Anniversary" boxed edition of Scrabble, some fishing lures (as seen on TV!), a tasteful area rug displaying dogs playing poker, a party-sized box of mesquite-flavored breakfast bars, a smart, faux-zebra occasional table (inlaid with a velvet depiction of different dogs playing poker), a tin of antacid tablets to help counteract having scarfed down a half-cooked hot dog at nine in the morning, an adhesive-backed closet light that plays show tunes, six army surplus road flares (you never know), a bag of ferret repellant, a back-up spare set of Scrabble tiles (you never know), a set of "Bewitched" themed picnic paper plates (featuring both Darrins), four paving stones, an emergency kit of cat-leg splints, and a solar-powered microwave oven.

And a twenty-four-pack of tube socks.

Who Ever Thought We'd Miss Nixon?

** Politics: The Song (and dance) Remains The Same **

Uncle Sam, Inc.

(For this employment exam, I think you're supposed to cheat.)

"Well, we can't *all* work for the government."

Remember that joke our dads used to make? Ha ha.

I remember those days. Well, a little. Mostly, I remember watching Laura Petrie wearing Capri pants on *The Dick Van Dyke Show.* I remember having feelings for Laura similar to those that MSNBC reporters say they have for Barack Obama.

But lately, it seems nobody in America is hiring *except* the government. In fact, the only non-governmental sector that's surviving is a small scrum of motels along the Indiana state line. And *they're* only hanging on because they're booked solid with holed-up politicians from places like Illinois, Wisconsin, and Yemen, who are hiding out so they won't have to do anything risky, like make a budget, or vote.

"But we can't *all* work for the government." Ha ha. Ha ha ha.

In California, there are now approximately 289 skillion people on the state's payroll. And those 289 skillion government employees have a guaranteed retirement, plus unlimited Capri pants.

But they don't make anything. They don't build anything. They all have to paid by people who make stuff - the "private sector." And there are only three people left in California who actually make stuff. (The stuff they make is payroll software ... guess who buys the software.)

You see where it leads. The math's not that tricky. Eventually, for every five government employees who are promised a pension, there will be an underlying supporting work force of ... well, of zero. Nobody. Nobody's left, and nobody has to pay for everybody.

Ultimately, the pyramid flips. And didn't Bernie Madoff just go to prison for "opportunities" like that?

Still, if nobody's hiring but our odd Uncle, we've limited options. It only makes sense that we all hop on the Public Sector gravy train - except for that whole "there's no money" thing. But we'll worry about that later, eh, Bernie?

Ha ha ha ha ha ha ha.

And so, to help you prepare for your new career, let's take this quick twenty-question US Civics Quiz.

Ready?

Let's begin:

--~~--~~--~~--~~--~~

1) What kind of government does the United States have?
    a. A bisexual camera
    b. A bilateral ligature
    c. It's the illegitimate love child of Lady Liberty and Uncle Sam.
    d. The kind that hides in motel rooms

2) How many branches of government do we have?
    a. Three: the Head, the Thorax, and the Minutemen
    b. Three: the Gerald Ford, the Jerry Lewis, and the Gerrymander
    c. Two: the DMV and the IRS
    d. Three: the Executive, the Honeymoon, and the Queen-Size (ask about our breakfast bar!)

3) How many states do we have?
    a. Three: Awake, Asleep, and Tenured
    b. Does Arizona still count?
    c. According to the President, there are fifty-seven.
    d. How many states of what?

4) Who has the ability to declare war?
    a. John Wayne
    b. The President, but he has to tell Congress first, so they can go hide in a motel until after the vote.
    c. Any citizen can declare war, but they can't declare it in a crowded movie theatre.
    d. My ex-wife

5) Who becomes President if both the President and Vice President die?

a. The Speaker of the Senate. After that, we all take turns.
b. I think it depends on what inning we're in.
c. Frank Sinatra
d. Either one of the two Arlen Specters, but not both

6) Name one requirement a person must meet in order to be eligible to become President.

a. They should form an exploratory committee, whose job is to eat food at the Iowa state fair.
b. They should have had their soul surgically removed, and replaced with a camera-activated grin generator.
c. They should have been born, but that's not really a deal-breaker anymore.
d. Bucketloads of cash

7) What is the correct introduction to the Constitution?

a. The Free Amble
b. The Pentateuch
c. Four scores and something, something, followed by Christina Aguilera singing the National Antler
d. "Hello, Constitution."

8) What is the supreme law of the United States?

a. The Ten Demandments
b. The USS Constitution. Or the USS Enterprise. One of those.
c. Never send your fullback on a post pattern when the defense is showing blitz.
d. Do unto others before they do unto you.

9) What do we call a change to the Constitution?

a. A commencement
b. A long-overdue effort to get guns back on the streets, where they belong
c. A reason for yet another book from Glenn Beck
d. Judicial activism

10) What is the Bill of Rights?

a. A list of the 100 easiest companies to sue
b. Wait a minute! That's part of the driver's exam, isn't it?
c. All the stuff the Founding Fathers meant to include, but forgot, after Samuel Adams showed up with the lager wagon
d. An enumeration of inalienable rights, which made sense prior to a non-enumerated flood of illegal inaliens

11) The Constitution has how many Amendments?

a. Two per state, and they amend for six years
b. There are still ten, even though Moses dropped them.
c. Nobody knows for sure, cause the ACLU keeps hiring more lawyers.
d. If I count the Bill of Rights as one, can I use the Ten-Amendments-Or-Less lane?

12) The first ten Amendments to the Constitution are known as what?

a. Poor Richard's Almanac
b. The subject of Glenn Beck's last 875 books
c. America, Take Two
d. In some circles, they're called "optional."

13) Name one right guaranteed by the First Amendment.
    a. Basic cable
    b. The right to arm bears
    c. Hot Pockets
    d. The right to be offended and then march around in public holding up unbelievably misspelled signs

14) Which is part of the Judicial branch at the Federal level?
    a. Sonia Sotomayor and the Supremes, Greatest Hits, Volume II
    b. Laura Petrie and the Pips
    c. Tom Petty and the Tortbreakers
    d. We don't have any Jews at the Federal level.

15) Who selects the Supreme Court justices?
    a. Now that Simon's gone, Randy and J Lo, I guess
    b. The legal firm managing the estate of Diana Ross
    c. Some guy in Georgetown who sells black robes on eBay
    d. Whoever wins "First Monday in October" Bingo Night at the Old Justices' Retirement Home

16) How many Supreme Court justices are there?
    a. Two per state, and they justify for six years
    b. Five. A soprano, alto, tenor, and bass, plus one extra alto, to handle tie-breakers.
    c. How many are there *where*?
    d. Let's see: there's Grumpy, Sneezy, Dopey, Doc ...

17) Why are there 100 Senators in the Senate?
    a. Early Massachusetts prisons could only house 100 felons at a time.
    b. Some kind of Y2K computer glitch

c. We're not really sure, but here's a clue: "100 bottles of beer on the wall..."
d. The Founders couldn't imagine any more zeros; else, we'd now have fourteen trillion Senators.

18) How many full terms may a Senator serve?

a. One at a time. Then they have to get re-indicted.
b. Depends. How much money they got?
c. Fifteen-to-twenty, with time off for good behavior
d. Where did you get this confused idea that they actually *serve?*

19) Which of the following is *not* an enumerated right granted to members of the US Congress?

a. Unusually odd faces and hairstyles (this is not an enumerated right, but it sure does keep happening)
b. The right to vote on stuff you can't pronounce, like "nucular" energy
c. The right to hide investments in the stock market, to hide real estate in Aruba, or to hide out in an Indiana motel room
d. Your wallet (although an Amendment is being considered)

20) When two or more Senators approach an intersection, who has the right-of-way?

a. Whichever Senator has managed to get the intersection named after her/him
b. The one who's farthest to the left
c. Whoever's in the pocket of the paving company
d. It's a moot point. There are no intersections in Aruba.

--~~--~~--~~--~~--~~

BONUS QUESTION

21) Name one benefit derived from US membership in the United Nations.

a. You asked us that last week. We're still stumped.
b. You're kidding, right?

--~~--~~--~~--~~--~~

Well, there it is, then. Hope you enjoyed our little quiz! And good luck with your career in Civil Service!

(For a list of Indiana motel phone numbers, send $25 to the Laura Petrie museum, 100 Capri Lane, Aruba.)

Big Teeth

(An ugly analysis of history's most expensive beauty contest)

Well, we've logged another Election Day for the history books. Unless the revisionists have already rewritten this year's history books.

President Dude appeared simultaneously at rallies in, as Joe Biden might put it, "all fifty-five battleground states." The President looked both teleprompters in the eye and told everybody to be sure and vote, because all that change he promised two years ago had just been rescued from an Arizona Prison, where it had been held prisoner by George Bush.

"I was coming with it! Next week! Thursday, 3pm! I had the Change in a box and was gonna release it next week! Yes we can! Next Thursday! Yes we can!"

In truth, it was actually a fairly normal day in America. And that, if you think about it, is amazing. People were allowed to vote, our government adjusted itself accordingly (and without bloodshed), and there were no military forces involved before, during, or after. That's a normal day here.

As a wise guy who writes satire, I bark and snipe and make a lot of noise, but deep down, I'm very, very proud of my country, and of my countrymen.

Okay, now that we got *that* out of the way . . .

Here are some random scenes from Election Day, 2 November 2010. Witness:

- Holding a press conference in an California drug mule tunnel, Barbara Boxer announced that she had managed to get her remaining hair hired by Hewlett Packard, but the hair was then out-sourced to China by Carly Fiorina.
- Poll-watching activists sued South Dakota's Black Hills and White Plains, New York, citing irreconcilable racial differences. Brownsville, Texas and Yellow Jacket, Colorado had no comment.
- In a last-ditch effort to simplify the write-in ballot, Alaska's ego dragon, Lisa Murkowski, had her name legally changed to "A."
- 24x7 campaigning began to take its toll on some of the players. At a late-afternoon rally in Pennsylvania, Bill Clinton wagged his finger at the crowd and insisted that he had not had sex with himself.
- Hearing about Harry Reid's early lead in Nevada, MSNBC's Chris Matthews claimed he felt a tingling in his leg, but the tingle turned out to be Dennis Kucinich, stuck in Matthews' crew sock.

- In South Carolina, Jim DeMint appeared to be leading Al Green, although Green had appeared at a county fair, holding an action figure of himself and challenging DeMint's prize-winning honeybee collection to a Spelling Wasp.
- Based on early exit polling, Maryland's Barbara Mikulski looked to maintain her Senate seat after her hair and its hair spray threatened to swallow the "z" from her opponent's name. Mikulski promised to ingest several other consonants if necessary.
- Based largely on alleged "I used to be a witch" comments, Delaware's O'Donnell prepared to get beaten like an eight-egg omelet. When asked for proof that O'Donnell was a witch, celebrity double-figure Joy Behar, who was released on a day pass from Roswell, New Mexico by Barbara Walters, cried out, "she looks like one!" Behar also claimed that O'Donnell had turned her (Behar) into a newt. Of course, no one could argue with that.
- After hearing of O'Donnell's fond and growing fan base, Barbara Boxer issued a statement asking to be called a "warlock," because she had worked really hard, you know, to get there.
- Shortly thereafter, at several East Coast polling sites, New Black Panthers claimed they had been attacked by Winged Monkeys.
- During a Midwest rally, Sarah Palin sneezed so hard that her sinus cavities aired out for the first time in three decades, which cleared up her oddly-attractive nasal twang. This caused a surge in Palin's popularity among sado-masochistic West Coast liberals, causing Barbara Boxer to join Gold's Gym, where she worked, you know, really hard.

- Not to be outdone by Boxer, Nancy Pelosi flew her private jet from Northern Orange County to Southern Orange County and went shopping for a leather gavel.
- In a small Rhode Island town, fourteen citizens simultaneously walked east, causing the state to tilt to the right. FoxNews immediately issued a new graphic, and three ACORN poll-watchers sued a conservative filmmaker they found hiding in a closet. ACORN then sued the closet, citing irekoncil ... orreconc ... ireckonsi ... winged monkeys.
- Based on an odd statistical anomaly, all gubernatorial candidates in Texas were exactly even in the polls, so they all shot each other. Austin, the state capital, immediately relocated to Ciudad Juarez and made a vampire movie with George Clooney and Quentin Tarantino, starring Lex Luthor as Jerry Brown.
- In South Carolina, Hey Hey Nikki Haley Barber decided to join a Monck's Corner nunnery (or a Nun's Corner monkery) and had to give up her corn-cob-filled flatbed truck. Her opponent Vincent Price Charlie Sheen prematurely went to his victory party, but was tragically killed by a Maurice's Barbecue sandwich that was stuffed in the underwear of a rogue exchange student from Fiji. The Department of Homeland Security promised to profile the student and immediately begin searching the underwear of all tourist-class grandparents, looking for any suspicious printer toner cartridges.
- In Pennsylvania, Joe Sestak's teeth won, when challenger Pat Toomey's teeth were run over by an Amtrak commuter train conducted by Joe Biden's fifty-five teeth.
- In Florida, Marco Rubio had to withdraw after he was mistaken for a short pile of something white. Then,

tragically, he got snorted in a large Miami mansion by Michelle Pfeiffer and Al Pacino, starring Mel Gibson as Nick Nolte.

- Liberal challenger Kendrick Meek also ducked out of the Florida race after accepting a TV offer. Meek changed his name to Butch von Andros and plans to star as Barbara Boxer in a reality show with Monica Lewinski and Vernon Jordan, tentatively called "Miami Vice Grip."
- At several Palm Beach County polling sites, winged monkeys claimed they had been attacked by angry AARP members in golf carts, who pelted the monkeys with filed-down purple heartburn tablets.
- And Florida's Charlie "I'm too tanned to work" Crist could not be reached for comment, as he and Arlen Specter were busily fine-tuning a sweet new Shape-Shifter mechanical toy that they bought at Faust 'R' Us.

Yep. A fairly normal day in America.

We, the Other People

(13 stars, right? No, wait. 13 stripes. Right? No, wait.)

The 2010 Census statistics are in, and they are fascinating. I'll give you a quick clue: the statistics were published in Spanish.

Now, I don't think it will come as any great huge surprise to learn that American demographics are changing. Just look at 1-800 numbers. These days, when you try to call somebody to get some help with something, you first have to sift through about three dozen language options.

- "To continue in Canadian, press one."
- "To continue in Spanish, marque dos."
- "To be seriously insulted by our staff, please enter your area code."
- "For moderate-to-light insults, please enter your grandmother's Social Security Number."
- "For no insults at all, please call back during abnormal business hours."
- "For a copy of your instruction manual, press nine. Please choose between an utterly unreadable carbon copy, or one written by hand in an obscure North Korean dialect."

- "To continue in Latin, press IV."
- "To continue in French, please stop pressing the bell, please!"
- "To continue in North Carolina, holler."
- "To continue in Mandarin, call your member of Congress and tell 'em to keep spending."
- "To speak to someone who speaks English, please call someone in India."

But we're still who we've always been, if you define "always" as "a couple dozen decades." We're still America, unless you're talking about our debt. Or our jobs. We're still Americans, unless your land is being confiscated under Eminent Domain. Or has been foreclosed. Or is situated near a nuclear reactor. Or a fault line. Or both.

At our core, or corazon, we're still the same melting olla.

So let's stay true to our principles. Let's stay prepared. Let's hold to our rich history, cause our history is pretty much the only thing left that's *allowed* to be rich. Let's cherish our history books.

And quickly, before the Fact Police finish rewriting those, too, let's take this quick 20-question US History Quiz.

Ready? Let's begin:

--~~--~~--~~--~~--~~

1) What is the name of the ship that brought the Pilgrims to America?

a. The Mayday
b. The Wallflower

c. There were three: the el Nino, the Ford Pinto, and the Ave Maria.
d. Allied Moving Vans

2) Why did the Pilgrims come to America?
   a. In England, they had to deal with religious incontinence.
   b. They were searching for an earlier group: the lost colony of Motown.
   c. So they could wear great big hats, monstrous buckles, knee socks and knickers, but avoid all the snide remarks.
   d. They were looking for a trade route to Indiana.

3) Who helped the Pilgrims in America?
   a. The Cleveland Indians
   b. Dick Clark
   c. Onomatopoeia, a native American who was pretty smart, except he kept calling corn "maize."
   d. That Aflac duck

4) What is the title of our National Anthem?
   a. The Star-Spangled Anthem
   b. The Hokey-Pokey
   c. Moon River
   d. Christina Aguilera's Transient Ischemic Attack

5) Who was known as the "Father of our Country?"
   a. George Washington Irving
   b. Those rascally Kennedys
   c. Dick Clark
   d. Wilt Chamberlain

6) Who was the chief writer of the Declaration of Independence?

a. George Washington
b. Steven Spielberg
c. Poor Richard Petty
d. George and Louise Jefferson

7) What holiday was celebrated for the first time by the American colonists?

a. Codependence Day
b. Indian Summer
c. The shopping day after Thanksgiving
d. The Daytona 500

8) What do we celebrate on Independence Day?

a. The Fourth of July
b. The invention of the firecracker
c. Cinco de Mayo
d. Life, liberty and the pursuit of happiness. Or barbecue. Same thing.

9) Where does "freedom of speech" come from?

a. Oprah
b. Robin Hood and the Magnum Charter
c. The larynx
d. Divorce

10) Which countries were our enemies during the War of 1812?

a. Eighteen hundred and eleven other countries
b. Ontario and the other Great Lakes
c. The Klingons
d. The Romulans

11) Which countries were our enemies during World War II?
   a. Foreign countries
   b. Volkswagen, Toyota and Ferrari
   c. The Axle of Evil
   d. Both the Klingons *and* the Romulans

12) Who was Susan B. Anthony?
   a. She was a fighter for a woman's right to vote, but I forget which woman.
   b. She was the wife of that Roman guy, Marc Anthony.
   c. She fought for women's suffering jets.
   d. She invented the quarter.

13) What is the name of the President's official home?
   a. General Electric
   b. The Caucasian-American House
   c. I think it was Indonesia. Or Kenya.
   d. Expedia

14) What is the proper title of the head of a city government?
   a. Mr. Head
   b. Clint Eastwood
   c. Jean Valjean
   d. My city where I live? My cousin, Tony.

15) What is the capital of the US?
   a. George Washington Irving
   b. An undisclosed, high-security bank in Peking
   c. Well, idiot. There's a capital "U" and then there's a capital "S." Like, duh.
   d. Right now, it's probably about eight bucks.

16) Where does Congress meet?
  a. In Congress. (Sounds like an answer they'd give, huh?)
  b. In a lobby, or a hearing, or an indictment, or prison, or witness protection programs, or a caucus.
  c. In locations that are critical to American security, like Aruba.
  d. Sometimes they meet people in public bathrooms. Makes you wonder what "caucus" means, eh?

17) What is the historical significance of "Remember the Alamo?"
  a. The birthplace of Willie Nelson
  b. It was the first car rental company discovered by Lewis and Clark.
  c. It's where Davy Crockett used David Bowie's knife and killed him a barmaid when he was only three. But he was still charged as an adult.
  d. It was the last time any American officials actually tried to enforce border security.

18) Who is the current President of the United States?
  a. Oh. Marvin...um...um. Aw, what's his name? Charlie Sheen's dad.
  b. Some Irish guy. Brock O'Something.
  c. That guy on, you know, on "24." Whaddayacallit. Used to make Allstate commercials.
  d. General Electric

19) Who is the current Vice President of the United States?
  a. Bono
  b. Rom D. Manuel
  c. George Carlin, I think. That white-haired guy who swears all the time.

d. Vice? Bill Clinton, I guess.

20) What is the official language of the United States?
  a. JavaScript
  b. German Chocolate
  c. Emoticons
  d. Greed

--~~--~~--~~--~~--~~

BONUS QUESTION

21) Name one benefit derived from US membership in the United Nations.
  c. You're kidding, right?
  d. Right?

--~~--~~--~~--~~--~~

Well, there it is, then. Hope you enjoyed our little quiz!

Next week, we'll be bringing you a little quiz about the US Constitution and the structure of American government. So you've got a whole week to go hide.

Me, I'm gonna go watch a Marvin Sheen movie and have some microwaved pop-maize.

Too Good To Be False

(No, it's not just you. We're confused over here, too.)

Let's play a game.

Let's just stop for a minute. Cause we need a break. If you're like me, you try to keep up with the news. And if you're at all like me, you've spent way too much time over the last few weeks questioning your own hearing, if not your own sanity. You hear something on the news, and the sheer weight of hammering nonsense hits you between the shoulder blades. It breaks down your motor control. You lock up. You stand, rooted, staring at the TV, mouthing the words, "Oh no, he didn't" or "She did NOT say that."

So let's play a game. Here's how it works. For each actual news item below, I've listed some intensely stupid scenarios. Your job is to digest the digests and try to pick out the one that, staggeringly stupid or not, actually happened.

LEGAL DISCLAIMERS

You should not take this quiz while operating heavy machinery. There is some seriously stupid stuff here. Especially the parts that are true.

You should not focus on this quiz for more than a few minutes at a time. Prolonged exposure to this much stupidity could result in an irrepressible desire to start writing television sitcoms.

Ready? Let's begin.

US Politics: Economy

Facing benefit cuts, thousands of unionized surgeons in Wisconsin went on strike, refusing to perform life-saving operations. However, in their defense, many of them walked around a lot, holding up signs saying "I'm only doing this because I 'heart' my patients so much." Meanwhile, thousands of their patients died. But that's okay; after all, *the patients weren't even in a union!*

-~~--~~--~~-

To avoid voting on budget proposals that could take away jobs, especially their *own* jobs, one of the political parties in the Wisconsin legislature ran away, to hide in a hotel in another state. Just ... ran away. During a recorded interview, one of those adults who ran away to hide in a hotel insisted that, by running away and hiding in a hotel, he was "standing up for the people."

-~~--~~--~~-

Wisconsin's Governor passed an emergency resolution requiring that nobody be allowed to loiter in the Capitol Rotunda unless they were, in fact, rotund.

-~~--~~--~~-

The Academy Awards

Both of this year's "Best Supporting" winners showed their gratitude, and their elegant, timeless Tinseltown style, by cursing in front of a billion viewers on live TV.

-~~--~~--~~-

James Traficant, the former Ohio Congressman, was honored in a "lifetime achievement" award when his hairstyle was retroactively awarded an Oscar for Best Special Effect In A Horror Movie.

-~~--~~--~~-

In a real nail-biter, Mel Gibson's temper narrowly edged out Joan Crawford's temper for Best Short Subject.

-~~--~~--~~-

As in previous years, Woody Allen refused to appear at Hollywood's top gala. And as in previous years, nobody much cared.

-~~--~~--~~-

US Culture

A citizen of San Francisco circulated a petition to ban circumcisions in the Bay Area. (I guess we should've seen that coming, once they outlawed Happy Meals.) We say "citizen" because, frankly, we couldn't tell which of Frisco's six available genders this particular meddler had selected. There was facial hair present, but these days, that doesn't rule out much except, maybe, mollusks.

-~~--~~--~~-

In February, Americans celebrated President's Day, a day when we honor all our former Presidents, because it took every single one of them, combined, to equal the debt piled up in only two years by this current President.

-~~--~~--~~-

In response to high demand for the "morning after" pregnancy-ending drug known as Plan B, federal promiscuity experts (a division of IRS Health Services) approved a pill to remove all traces of personal responsibility. The new drug will be marketed under the trade name Noplanitol.

-~~--~~--~~-

US Politics: Elections

In Chicago's contentious election for Mayor, voter turnout was quite heavy. According to early exit polling, Rahm Emanuel led in fifty-one of the city's forty-three voting districts.

-~~--~~--~~-

Chicago poll-watchers were at a loss to explain the appearance of over 12,000 Wisconsin schoolteachers, whose voter registration cards had "Wisconsin" crossed out and the words "registered Chicago voter" penciled in.

-~~--~~--~~-

According to reports, a Chicago voter who looked like Sean Connery was allegedly gunned down by a voter who looked like Robert de Niro. The gunman was eventually brought to justice by a voter who looked like Kevin Costner. Shortly thereafter, Prohibition was repealed.

-~~--~~--~~-

One week before the election, three investigative reporters who were investigating the Chicago political machine mysteriously vanished. In an unrelated story from London, Madame Tussauds Wax Museum announced a new exhibit featuring three Chicago investigative reporters.

-~~--~~--~~-

Ultimately, despite niggling details like not technically living there, Rahm Emanuel was elected Mayor of Chicago.

-~~--~~--~~-

World Events

In Libya, Colonel Qaddafi stood on somebody's balcony and spoke for sixty-one hours. He eventually completed a sentence, though this is unconfirmed. During his address, Qaddafi shook his fist at the world, insisting that he would never leave the country until he had worn every single hat in his expansive hat collection. Qaddafi then demanded that somebody bring him a "u" to follow the "q" in his name.

-~~--~~--~~-

In a report from CNN's bureau somewhere in the Pakistani Kush, Usama bin Laden publicly surrendered. Unfortunately, his speech was translated by Christine Aguilera, resulting in US Intelligence laying down air strikes on an undisclosed area they called the Cushion of Pac-Man.

-~~--~~--~~-

The United Nations convened to ponder the worsening situation in the Middle East. After several days of free meals, the UN council issued a non-binding resolution, confirming that they were all really, really unhappy and stuff.

-~~--~~--~~-

Colonel Qaddafi, wearing a wool hat with earflaps and decked out in a strapless Donna Karan number, blamed the Libyan revolution on al Qaeda. Middle East analysts commented on how refreshing it was to find something that's not George Bush's fault.

-~~--~~--~~-

Finally facing the Libyan situation, President Obama took decisive action by sending Hillary to Geneva. That way, if Colonel Qaddafi ever happens to show up in Switzerland, Hillary will have already scored the best table in the restaurant.
Take THAT, terrorists!

-~~--~~--~~-

Well, I hope you enjoyed our little diversion. I'm sure we'll talk again ... after all, it's only February.

One more comment: if those Frisco meddlers should succeed with that anti-circumcision petition, we can only hope they don't try to make it retroactive. Imagine the scene:

Unionized Health Care professional at the IRS: "Mr. Parham, we're gonna have to put it back."
Me: "Rave on, Jekyll."
(rushing, Barry-like sound, followed by door slamming)

Courting the Zombie Caucus

(To politicians, you're never dead. You're just re-targeted as an oxygen-deferred undecided.)

Even dead, he wouldn't shut up.

"Could be worse, I suppose," reasoned the corpse, riffling through his Food Stamps as he signed over his Stimulus check. "At least I'm not overweight."

He grinned at the grocery clerk. At least, I think it was a grin. "What's *your* name, dearie?"

"Perfect," I grumbled to myself. "Just perfect. Friday afternoon, I'm in a hurry. I glide into the Ten Items Or Less lane with two items. Two. But first, this stiff's gotta share his entire afterlife's story with Miffy The Checkout Clerk."

I must have a gift. No matter where I go - the bank, the pharmacy, the movie concession, the grocery, the post-tattoo hepatitis booster-shot clinic - I seem to have a knack for picking the slowest possible queue. But this was the first time I'd ever been stuck behind a member of the post-mortem public who was on government assistance.

And then it got worse. Miffy asked Bone Boy for some ID.

Some days, I just have no luck at all. I'd finally made it to a Friday without the need to recall any exploding Chinese products. Without any workplace distractions that included the words "disgruntled employee" and "hail of gunfire." So far, so good. But then, on the drive home from work, my new alternatively-fueled car from General Tso Motors, the Chrysler "Commune," ran out of sunshine. Fortunately, there was a Unionized road crew nearby taking a marijuana and beer break. The work gang heard my frustrated swearing, assumed I was filming a pro-Union political smear ad, and blazed me a quick "exit ramp to nowhere." That got me off the freeway, and I angled the Commune toward a nearby patch of sunlight. So far, so good.

But then I get stuck in the grocery express lane behind a dead guy on the dole.

So what's with all these casketeers cashing government checks? How did this happen? I'm sure you heard the news. Those clabber-skulled, clueless clowns in Washington ... the same mullet-heads who intend to attend to your internal organs ... somehow, they managed to mail seventy-two thousand Stimulus checks to seventy-two thousand dead people. Whoa. There's a staggering stupidity going on inside that beltway. This is world-class incompetence. I mean, a snafu of this magnitude gives a whole new meaning to the phrase "post-dated check."

Seventy-two thousand checks, mailed to people who, like Arlen Specter, no longer matter. The *good* news is that about half of the Stimulus checks were returned by people who, unlike Arlen Specter, are intellectually honest. But that brings us to the *bad* news: some thirty-six thousand Stimulus checks, apparently sent to zombies with a zip code, were *not* returned. I don't want to get into the eschatological issues involved, but this means that, somewhere, we've got a huge Michael Jackson "Thriller" video just waiting to happen.

(By the way, an additional seventeen thousand Stimulus checks were sent to incarcerated felons, too. But, fortunately, they were all sent to the same prison that housed co-felon Bernie Madoff. Bernie showed up with a shiv and a prospectus and, before anyone knew what had happened, he had "diversified" all the other convicts. Suddenly, there was a blood-curdling shriek, a giant whooshing sound, and celebrity attorney Gloria Allred swooped in. She's now representing the felons.)

So now you're probably wondering, like a good, obedient, 21st century robot: how can I get in on some of this free money? How do I get dead, and live to tell about it?

Well, if you're not dead already, there are plenty of ways to speed things up. You could smoke. You could hit yourself repeatedly with a stick, but that could take a while. You could stand on the Arizona-Mexico border waving a bogus work visa, or a gram of cocaine. You could go quail hunting with Dick Cheney. You could walk into a West Texas biker bar wearing a full-body tangerine leotard and shout, "I'm gay and I'm here to take your guns!" You could stand between Kim Jong-Il and a lunch buffet, or Arlen Specter and a microphone.

Hey, I'm just saying. You have options.

Here's another idea for simply ceding all personal control and letting the government pay you to die. Ever considered combining government Food Stamps with utterly negligent, staggeringly gross obesity? Lots of people are! And with a record forty-one million people now shopping for food with Food Stamps instead of their own money, a big behind can't be far behind.

Every day on TV, you can hear dozens of extremely emaciated, irritating experts, warning that Americans (to use the highly-technical medical terminology) are like really way large and stuff. In fact, according to one report, Americans are getting so morbidly overweight that, by the year 2020, 2 out of 3 people will be 3 out of 4 people.

Come to think of it, the ultimate "free government money" solution may be staring us in the face. After all, we're only discussing the bat-biscuit insanity that we *know about* in Washington, concerning felons and Food Stamps and formerly breathing people. There's *no telling* how much Stimulus money they might be sending to dead overweight convicts.

And, of course, you could've just simply starved to death, waiting behind this dead schmuck last Friday at the grocery, who acted like he's the first ex-person in history to ever be asked for some ID.

So frustrating, this guy. I coulda re-killed him.

How To Survive A Government Shutdown

(a publication of the Dept. of Government Shutdown Survival)

Welcome to the Federal Government! Now, take the rest of the week off!

Ha ha ha. Wasn't that fun? That was an example of internal government humor, as approved by the Federal Agency For Chuckles And Giggles. (guffaws are handled by another agency)

Seriously, though, the purpose of this publication is to provide you with guidance and support, in the unlikely event of a government shutdown. But first, let's get some legal housekeeping out of the way.

PUBLICATION METADATA: This document supersedes all previous documents issued by this department that we printed earlier, we think, though maybe not, although we definitely did pay people to print them earlier, although maybe they didn't get around to it, but we're fairly certain that, in any case, we wrote them a check for printing the documents as they were described in the print specification. That was the plan, anyway.

DISCLAIMER: This is the revised revision of the latest revision, revised by the Modifications And Revisions Sub-Committee of the Ad Hoc Revisions Task Force, by order of the sitting manager of the standing Revisions Action Group, as authorized by the pro tem co-chairs of the Department of Revised Modification Revisions, duly approved by the Federal Council of Seriously Important Government Employees Who Are Utterly Essential No Matter What.

REVISED DISCLAIMER: It may have come as a surprise to you to discover that there *is* a Department of Government Shutdown Survival - an entire bloated bureaucracy that exists for no other reason than to issue pamphlets about what the government should do when the government's not doing anything. Not to worry. If you (or someone you know) is surprised, please visit the Department of Surprise Management's website, a resource maintained by the Federal Incredulity And Disbelief Management Agency, where you will discover reams of "Dealing With Surprise In The Federal Workspace" documents, many of them staggeringly ironic.

Thanks for reading the metadata and disclaimers! Now, take the rest of the week off! *Ha ha.*

Seriously, though, there are many benefits to working for the American people:

- The life-long security of a federal government job
- Hubris

- The character-building challenge of obtaining security clearance for the bathroom
- Guest appearances on C-SPAN, or "America's Most Wanted"
- That warm, fulfilling feeling that comes from being referred to as "non-essential"
- The heady rush of living under the ever-looming threat of a legal indictment
- Knowing that the ideal candidate is not technically required to be awake, conscious, or in special cases, alive (see Appendix G: "flex-work" opportunities)
- The Witness Protection Program

So government employment is a plum that draws the eye of many perspective job-seekers! Unfortunately, government employment may also draw the attention of nosy reporters, pesky watch groups, and ungrateful whistle-blowers. It's not their fault - these are nattering factions that can't shake their ingrained, narrow-minded worldview which still confuses "job" with "work." These are very small, petty, extremely dull people. It's not their fault.

But, as federal employees, we know better. We were not put on this planet to work; no, our purpose is to get paid. *Period.* And that's where the problem begins.

See, sometimes, due to orgiastic spree-based spending, or mind-boggling levels of bureaucratic incompetence, the federal government will run out of money. And as we've pointed out, we don't park our tenured tushies in these federal cubicle farms - sometimes as often as three days a week - just because we love America. *We're here to get paid.* And even those violent kittenstranglers in the Tea Party will understand that, in order to pay people, you have to have some money.

But the general public just doesn't get it. They act like the government works for *them*, or something.

It's not their fault.

But there are very personal, very real ramifications of a government shutdown, as can be seen from the following list, compiled during the 2011 shutdown showdown by the non-partisan Non-Numbered Bullet-List Generation Sub-Committee, as commissioned by the Federal Department of Formatted Vertical Statistics And Agenda List Items Presented Without Emoticons:

- In the case of a shutdown, travelers might not be able to get a passport or a visa. (This only applies to legal citizens who are planning a trip *outside* America - any fool can get *in* to America)
- The President of the United States warned that the District of Columbia might have to ... now hold on to something ... cancel the Cherry Blossom Parade. Then he flew to Brazil, and then to California, and then Rome, then Chicago and Iowa, then Rome again, then back to Brazil, to read a speech outlining why Americans ought to be conserving fuel.
- The Tea Party was accused of fomenting the entire "shutdown" crisis. They were also accused of causing tectonic shift, funding the Spanish Inquisition, and creating lactose intolerance.
- In the case of a shutdown, national parks might have to close. According to Al Gore, some of them might even

explode. The White House noted that this could save or create eighteen million jobs making disaster movies.

- Senator Charlie Rangel noticed a microphone, which meant he had to start talking, and then he made the confusing comment that "cutting spending doesn't mean you're saving money." However, before he could begin his next sentence, his ego took a direct hit from an incoming Absurdity Bomb From Outer Space. The ego survived.
- In the case of a shutdown, C-SPAN might have to show reruns. The White House noted that this could save or create eighteen million jobs filling anti-depression prescriptions.
- Hearing about the national parks, Smokey the Bear took his own life. Senator Harry Reid blamed the Tea Party, and pointed out that John Boehner now has the blood of an imaginary federal employee on his hands. In an unrelated story, McGruff the Crime Dog went missing. Harry Reid says he fears the worst. The Attorney General subpoenaed the Tea Party's phone records, and the President of the United States said that McGruff had "acted stupidly."
- In the case of a shutdown, Pentagon budget cuts might force the military to discontinue not fighting the non-war that we're not currently not fighting, but not in Libya. And a shutdown could cause US airport security to have to rein in and rely on the "honor system."
- A shutdown could even affect the critical, sacred duties of the leader of the free world. Rather than ride the course in Golf Cart One, the President of the United States might have to walk the entire eighteen holes.
- The Tea Party was blamed for childhood poverty, people who wear plaid shorts and black knee socks, and the fate of millions of minority senior citizens who died prior to the War of 1812. And during. And since.

- As the Shutdown Clock ticked down to Zero Hour, Senator Harry Reid got more and more agitated, until finally he rent his garment and gnashed his dentures. (Actually, he had a non-essential government employee clock in and proxy-rend her garment. Of course, this was a Federal Employee union-sanctioned activity, so there had to be three backup non-essential proxies, a Garment Rending Supervisor, and a follow-up performance review.)
- The Tea Party was blamed for the death of a German polar bear named Knut, the lack of air on Mars, and accused of injecting LDL cholesterol into defenseless Saturday morning cartoon characters.
- Smokey's funeral was very low-key and Spartan, what with the lack of cherry blossoms. Flags couldn't be flown at half-staff, because half-staff flag management is a Federal Employee union-sanctioned activity, under the auspices of the Federal Department of Kinda-High-But-Not-All-The-Way-Up Symbol Positioning Management.
- Due to vital international commitments, and a conflicting tee time, the President of the United States couldn't attend the funeral. However, reading from tandem teleprompters positioned somewhere on somebody's 12th fairway, he did recite some comforting anecdotes about Smokey, Yogi and Boo-Boo, and then, for some reason, pointed out that America had no better ally in the Middle East than Ireland. Next, the President re-tasked NASA with some kind of Ursa Outreach program, designed to make bears feel better about their historical contributions to jet propulsion, not to mention pic-a-nic baskets. Then he authorized the Pentagon to invade Yellowstone.
- An unnamed spokesperson from the Federal Department of Clandestine Opposition Management And Anonymous

Dissing blamed the Tea Party for the concept of three-dimensional space, and accused them of injecting Burmese termites into retirement homes while hitting unwary teachers with a partisan pointed stick.

- At the eleventh hour, a frantic Senator Harry Reid called an emergency press conference to share his concerns that he could see no way forward. Fortunately, though, a Senate page took charge, turning the Senate leader's chair around so that he wasn't facing the wall.
- Joe Biden pointed out that anybody can run into a wall and then, for a few minutes, cursed in a bipartisan way.
- The White House said they stood behind the Senate leader, but that just confused him again, so they stood in front of him.
- And then, at two minutes till midnight, Jack Bauer appeared! He hovered over the Capitol rotunda in a black helicopter theory! Chloe transmitted the schematics of Harry Reid's chair and the coordinates of three nearby mature people, who were in town for the Cherry Blossom Parade! And with adult supervision, the shutdown was averted!

Happy endings! Well, almost. Less than an hour later, after everybody forgot about the budget again, the President of the United States handed Jack over to the Chinese. As collateral.

Welcome to the Federal Government.

Now - take the rest of the week off!

Ha ha ha!

Lame Duck Soup

(Late 2010. Not exactly America's best day. Or month. Okay, year. Okay...)

I guess it was about 8:30 in the morning when I finally forced myself out of bed. I padded toward the shower, tapping the TV along the route. Fourteen car commercials later, the news blared back on. President Firefly was just wrapping his fourth speech of the day.

"I have just brokered a deal to sell American cars to South Korea, since we all know how Asians line up by the millions, clamoring to buy those heavy, clumsy, inefficient, Union-ruined junk-buckets that are turned out in Detroit using other people's money. And lo, I saw this deal, and it was good. We know this to be true, because I said it. This will save or create 130 million jobs. Pulling this off was not easy; that's why *I* had to do it, instead of letting you humans handle it. You're welcome. Now: rise, my people."

The television blinked and auto-cranked the volume knob. Six car dealers yelled at me about selling me a car for less than they paid for it, and then the volume re-regulated and we were back for the political "response" to the "Korean deal" from the "other side of the aisle." A tall, air-brushed orange-ish man with sad, weeping eyes adjusted his dark, presumptive, soon-to-be-Leader suit. He focused his gaze, for some reason, on someone off-camera, and then spoke.

"I have always been on record as being firmly on the record. Make no mistake. At the end of the day, I support exactly those things which the American people think they know I thought they asked me to think about supporting. Cause when the rubber hits the road, you can ask a horse to get you a drink, but you can't change streams in the middle of the game. And, as I've always said, you can take that to the bank."

I had now been awake for some seven minutes, so I knew what was coming next.

"This is a FoxNews Alert. WickedLeaks founder, the evil calculating Trentino, has announced the existence of another new secret file. Trentino has threatened, if he's ever captured, to release this new file's secret password to his evil spies, Chico and Harpo. According to insiders, this file contains understandably guarded American embassy transcripts, as well as the secret recipe from Kentucky Fried Chicken.

"White House sources pooh-poohed the announcement, scoffing that America can't let itself be afraid of one guy who plunked down $35 for a website domain name, or one seditious military Private who shrugged off all his oaths of allegiance and then managed to dance right out of the Pentagon with a quarter of a million classified documents that, if made public, could spell the end of multi-national civilization as we know it."

Two car dealers announced the absolute last chance for me to buy this year's cars at $10,000 below dealer invoice, have my pets spayed or neutered, and get free dental care for life.

Channel-surfing for a bit, I landed on MSNBC, quoting Vice President Joe Biden as saying that he sees no reason to get all bunged up about Iran having access to patty-cake uranium. At a quickly ginned-up news conference, that puppy-eyed, air-brushed "aisle" guy and eighteen other potential 2012 Presidential candidates pointed out that it's "yellow-cake" uranium, and collectively observed that the Vice President may need to get an MRI, possibly once or twice a week. The Vice President's response was, let's say, intimate.

Since America apparently had no more of those pesky border security problems, President Slurpee sent the US Attorney General overseas to try and land the 2022 World Cup. Presumptive Air-Brush called this an "interesting tactic," saying, "Oh, yeah. Let's send America's chief Law Enforcement Officer to dicker about concessions and stadium parking." The White House pointed out that this bold, brilliant move would save or create 230 million jobs.

Vice President Biden pointed out that the Attorney General had to handle the delicate World Cup negotiations; after all, NASA was busy mentoring group hug therapy sessions on the Muslim street.

Meanwhile, seven minutes passed.

"This is a FoxNews Alert. WickedLeaks has announced the existence of something they call an "insurance" document, which they threaten to release if the website's Google Ads ranking drops below a favorable quintile. According to insiders, this cache contains the European Union's personal PIN, two genies, and an extremely irritated leprechaun."

Since unemployment was solved and America was so flush with cash, President Class Warfare called down to the First Garage, had Air Force One gassed up, stocked the First Snackbar, and then flew off on a surprise visit to Absurdistan. He had planned to meet with Absurdi President Humid Karseat, but Karseat had to cancel after he hurt his leg after tripping over a large suitcase full of his brother's opium money.

The White House confirmed that our President would be on the ground in Absurdistan for a grand total of three hours. The Pentagon confirmed that it costs approximately $150,000 per hour to operate Air Force One (plus snacks). And a Google / Rand McNally search confirmed that it's a twenty-five-hour round trip from Washington to Absurdistan and back. That's 3.7 million taxpayer dollars to pony up for, as a hauntingly familiar (and equally intelligent) TV show once put it, a "three hour tour."

Vice President Biden pointed out that this bold, brilliant move saved or created 3.7 million dollars in additional debt. The air-brush guy swept away a tear, pointed out that a three-hour Skype call would have cost only $2.16, and further noted that seven minutes had expired.

"This is a FoxNews Alert. WickedLeaks has leaked that they are holding secret documents they are calling a "poison pill," and threaten to release the documents if anyone visits their website and then clicks their browser's "Back" button. According to insiders, the documents contain Absurdistan's patty-cake launch codes and pictures of various Congressional house-pets, all caught in compromising positions."

Geraldo Rivera pointed out that the actual cost to operate Air Force One is more like $181 thousand per hour. The Pentagon haughtily sniffed, pointing out that it was well aware of the cost, but in the spirit of the holidays, the defense agency was giving the fact-strapped Administration a frequent liar discount.

Two car dealers, each dressed in X-mas red, both claimed to be the car dealer whose deep discounts most respectfully celebrated the birth of X. They then challenged each other to a duel, promising one free floor mat to the first twenty customers who notified the loser's next of kin. Both dealers invited customers to take advantage of their "family tree" plan, which deferred all payments until the birth of descendants three-to-five generations down the line.

In a C-SPAN tape roll, I overheard the outgoing leader of the lame duck Congress, reviewing the lame things going on there on the Hill: "Okay, let's see. We voted that we all like Joe Paterno, and we let Rangel babble on for a while about how unfair life is. Now, there was something ... something else we were supposed to ... something that w ... oh yeah! The economy!"

MSNBC reported an impressive breakthrough, a real "drain the swamp" victory: in a broad show of bipartisanship, Vice President Biden held a secret, closed-door tax cut meeting with a few select Democrats. White House sources claimed the meeting saved or created 330 million jobs. I listened for, oddly, just under seven minutes.

"This is a FoxNews Alert. WickedLeaks has confirmed that it hides a vast number of really, really top-secret documents they are calling The Doomsday Files. The web-based cyber-giant threaten to release the dastardly, double-naught spy documents if anyone outbids them on that first edition Beatles album collection at eBay. According to insiders, the Doomsday Files contain a trojan-activated bit of nanotechnology, a microscopic assassin that would trigger an unprecedented, immediate, world-wide Botox expiration, causing Nancy Pelosi's entire face to fall off."

Congress, forgetting what it forgot that it just forgot, decided to debate more serious matters: whether rule-breaker Charlie Rangel should get a simple public raspberry, a more censorious group noogie, or the full monty: be restricted, for a full weekend, to basic cable (taxpayer-funded basic cable, of course).

Three car dealers all claimed to be the Number One Sales Dealer in our spiral galaxy, and invited everyone down to enjoy a complimentary breakfast and four-year college education, plus a free Senator for everyone with approved credit.

The Charlie Rangel dress-down had barely begun, when news came out that Rangel, who just got busted for ethics violations, might now be guilty of ethics violations concerning the way he paid his ethics violations lawyers, who were defending him against ethics violations.

Following the wicked WickedLeaks leaks, the White House ordered a full review of security procedures, prompting several dozen more Republicans to announce their 2012 Presidential aspirations. Once they complete this timely security review, the White House plans to launch an investigation into rumors of a

Rebel army forming in Charleston, South Carolina, and then try to get confirmation that the Beatles may be disbanding.

And speaking of doomsday ...

One local car dealer announced that they're having Truck Month. Another announced their Year-End Sale. And all of it - the month, and the year, and the end-of-the-year - they all begin AND end this weekend.

I'm going back to bed. It's too much, too confusing. Is this that Mayan calendar that's supposed to kill everybody?

We Are The Walrus

(2010: The battle of the ballot rises to a new low)

All right. To help set the mood for a little discussion of the 2010 mid-term elections, I'll use an actual quote. Hang on to something. Ready?

"I can neither confirm nor deny the truth or non-truth of that alleged fact."

Whew.

I know, I know. Mind-numbing. You okay? You sure? All right, then. If you're still conscious, let's continue.

First, the good news: as an American, you still get to vote, unless you're in the military. Now, the bad news: as American voters, we're not exactly presented with a buffet of enticing entrees, are we? A whole lot of hash, rehashed and rehashed. There's just something rancid about the term "career politician."

"Why, welcome back, sir or madam. Good to see you again. Would you like Candidate A or the other Candidate A?"

Hmmm. Should you vote for the politician over here who will raise your taxes, or that politician over there who will raise your taxes? Hmmm. It's like opening a box of 200 crayons, only to find out that all 200 are labeled "Bronte Mid-Winter Depression."

Generally, our options tend to range somewhere between someone who is dishonest and self-serving, to someone who is just killing a little time in-between fraud charges, bribery indictments or some kind of deviancy investigation that involves non-voters, like Bangkok public school cheerleaders, or disgruntled farm animals. But according to the ongoing barrage of political ads, the differences between candidates are staggering. World-changing.

The candidates spend boatloads of money trying to out-awesome each other, while gasping in disbelief at the pure, raw evil of their respective opponents. And this "Oh yeah? Says you!" escalation, between creatures that otherwise appear to be all-growed-up adults, can be hilarious.

Witness:

"Senator, you need to man up."
"Oh yeah? Well, you're a really ugly woman."
"Oh yeah? Is that your real hair, or are you doing turf research for a putt-putt?"

The Story of O: In a tight New York Governor's race, candidate Rick Lazio dropped his bid against opponents Andrew Cuomo, Carl Paladino, Tony Soprano, Othello, Iago, Bilbo, Frodo and

Topo Gigio. Paladino threatened some bad mojo in his borough, prompting a de facto promo for Lazio by J-Lo and de Niro at the Apollo.

A study commissioned by the Obama administration's new Weather Czar determined that certain types of moisture in Republican-leaning states are granted an unfair advantage, and the White House called for another $30 billion to fund a new Precipitation Equalization program. As a result, hot states now take wetness from cold states, unless the water was a pre-existing condition. Joe Biden claimed that this move saved or created oh, around 370 million jobs or so, more or less.

In South Carolina, a gubernatorial candidate released a campaign ad showing her standing in the bed of an old truck, piled high with ears of corn, shaking hands with a few dozen smiling citizens who were apparently big fans of corn, or old trucks, or gubernats. Her opponent countered with an attack ad featuring a disgruntled tomato sandwich that had lost its health insurance.

Witness:

"Congresswoman, 87% of the time, you voted against the rights of water in the atmosphere to organize."

"Oh yeah? Well, 89% of the time, you voted twice."

"Oh yeah? Is that your face, or did your head get caught in a hay baler?"

In Maryland, a Democrat was accused of taking illegal campaign donations. The opposing Republican was then accused of taking hostages and robbing a bank. Joe Biden called a news conference and pointed out that the Republican had obviously lost his gruntle. The White House suggested that the hostages were planted by the Tea Party, causing Congress to immediately call for an investigation into Sarah Palin's clothing budget, after which the TARP Czar sent $84 billion to a Brazilian bank, selected at random.

In the Delaware Senate race, the Republican was accused of feeding her own grandmother to a Rastafarian coyote. Her spokesman argued that everybody makes silly choices in high school, and was quick to point out that the Democrat candidate once robbed an organ bank at midnight and then built a proto-human monster. Since the Delaware DMV was closed at the time, the monster could not be reached for comment. According to unconfirmed reports, the monster has since been promoted to Supervisor and has achieved tenure.

In this 2010 free-for-all, here's how gutter-scraping low the situation has gotten: in the California Governor's race, a male candidate (or someone on his staff) referred to his female opponent as a "politician." Then, for the next ninety-six consecutive hours, FoxNews breathlessly used the new expression "somebody said the P word" at least eighteen billion times. The National Organization for Women could not be reached for comment, since they were busy changing their stationery letterhead to read "The National Organization for Some Females, If They Support The Same Political Views That We Do." On ABC's popular morning talk show, "The View," the distaff co-hosts were so offended that Whoopi Goldberg publicly proposed marriage to Bill O'Reilly, an act which nearly caused Joy Behar to walk off a few pounds.

Witness:

"I should point out that my opponent has never balanced a budget."

"Oh yeah? Well, at least I was never arrested at a Shriners' convention while holding an otter and wearing a shepherd's outfit!"

"Oh yeah? Well, at least I never dug a pit and tossed in defenseless puppies while voting to inject radioactive isotopes into disabled firemen!"

This year, it seems to be a clear case of "throw 'em all out." Nobody's seat is safe, not even San Francisco's favorite frequent flyer, Nancy "Let them eat food stamps" Pelosi. A recent poll claimed to prove that Madame Loudspeaker is even less popular than British Petroleum. Upon hearing this news, BP immediately filed for dual citizenship, formed the Earl Grey Party, and is challenging Pelosi's House seat, running on an off-shore platform rebuilt by Halliburton and stress-tested by Joy Behar.

Given his plummeting approval ratings, nobody wants the President anywhere near their mid-term campaign, not even members of his own party. So the President has had to settle for taking extra vacations and making speeches at the United Nations, where he wowed the assembled diplomats by making several meaningful hand gestures and knowingly biting his lip during outbursts of fawning applause. He told the assembled nations that governments should reward hard work, not reckless risk-taking. He said this with a straight face (see "plummeting approval ratings").

Even the President's inner circle are bailing. One top advisor resigned to go run for Mayor of Chicago, but was stymied for a while by real estate issues back home. He had sublet his house, it seems, and now the tenant was refusing to vacate the premises. All ended well, though. According to the police report, the tenant died of natural causes after backing at high speed into eighteen bullets.

Witness:

"The people of our state deserve a whole lot of stuff. And I am a whole lot of stuff. Vote for me, and I'll give you a car and pay your mortgage."
"Oh yeah? If the people of our state choose to honor me with their vote, I'll make everyone taller and grant you the power to speak in several languages."
"Oh yeah? When I'm elected, trees will drip fungible currency, and nobody in our state will ever die, if they're registered with our Party."

And then it came. The "October Surprise." A document was unearthed that changed everything. To be specific, a birth certificate. And now we know.

The President of the United States is actually a ninety-four-year-old Eskimo woman named Tina.

Ooh, Baby, It's A Wild World Wide Web

** I Heard It Through The Grapevine (then I re-tweeted it) **

King Tut & the Cheeseheads

(Confused? Wait till you see the NEXT 5,000 years!)

You know that feeling? Too much information, too fast? I don't know about you, but I'm still trying to figure out exactly what happened where. Odd times, lately, in Egypt's capital (Madison) and in Cairo, the capital of Wisconsin. I think I got that right, but it's all pretty confusing.

It's been one of those weird times where, if you tried to watch the events unfold on the TV news, you actually ended up more confused than if you'd just left the TV off. And our Intelligence Community seemed more confused than us, if that's even mathematically possible. Hang on, and we'll try to distill it all for you.

First, protestors swarmed the streets in Egypt (or maybe it was Wisconsin). They were complaining about food, I think. Or pensions, maybe. Or freedom.

Now, right away, I'd noticed a potential problem with the protests that were popping up in Egypt. All the protesters were gathered in Cairo's Tahrir Square. But Tahrir Square's not a square ... it's round. That's never going to work! They need to go get some corners! Some edges! You can't hate people in a circle!

See, people in Wisconsin would never make such a mistake. Americans may not know much, but we know how to hate, and how to tailgate. And that's why all countries on Earth need to join the NFL.

Next, pro-whatever and anti-something-I-forget-already riots broke out in Egypt and other places, including Kuwait, Djibouti, Tunisia, Threenisia, Fournisia and a University of Wisconsin frat house. A museum, a popular micro-brewery, several historic buildings and a dorm's Laundromat were stormed and looted, resulting in several extremely indignant coeds, damage to four beer kegs, and the re-death of two mummies. Fortunately, the kegs were saved.

NBC reported that Egypt's President had resigned. FoxNews reported that Egypt's President had agreed to resign. CNN reported that Egypt's President had vowed never to resign. MSNBC reported that FoxNews had resigned. The Huffington Post reported that Glenn Beck had invaded Egypt. Local news teams reported that the Wisconsin state legislature had apparently resigned, and abdicated. Wisconsin's Governor was captured on camera, looking resigned.

As the situations worsened, the American President flew off to some place to stand in front of some things and read some stuff to some group, and to sneak a quick cigarette. The spokesman for the White House, who was himself about to resign, released the following, powerful, history-making statement: "Well, we'll just have to wait and see."

Due to a garbled miscommunication, US Intelligence issued a "fire at will" command, intended to take out any badger mascots or rogue Egyptian schoolteachers spotted north of Cairo, Illinois.

In a news fluff piece, Secretary of State Hillary Clinton fondly recalled the time she was trapped under heavy incoming fire at Kuwait's O'Hare airport.

Since it had been nearly ten minutes since his last speech, the American President flew off to some place, stood in front of some stuff, and read some advice: Egypt's President needed to "listen to the wishes of his citizens."

I nearly fell off the couch. That's like Richard Simmons chiding somebody for wearing gym shorts on national TV.

Egypt's President responded to the Wisconsin teacher strike by publicly beheading a badger. He then threatened to withhold much-needed food from those who continued to protest in the streets, and he began rationing beef. This was a clear case of despot culling the cattle back, and if you can think of a worse pun than *that*, you win.

Next, in Wisconsin, the theory is that thousands of schoolteachers simultaneously ate some bad egg salad, forcing them all to call in sick on the same day. The tainted egg salad also manifested as some form of mass psychosis in these truants, causing every single educator to stagger, like so many tenured zombies, down to the state capital, where they begin screaming out random verb conjugation exercises.

Due to a garbled miscommunication, US Intelligence recalled the entire Fifth Fleet from Bahrain, redeployed them down the Saint Lawrence Seaway, and enforced a blockade on the Erie Canal.

Back in the Middle East, an entire political party from Wisconsin defected to either Djibouti, or Illinois. They holed up in a Best Eastern hotel room, where they spent the rest of the weekend calling room service and demanding free, taxpayer-funded shawarmas, or at least some of those Hot Pocket thingies.

NBC announced that Egypt's President had left the country. FoxNews announced that he had refused to leave the country. CNN announced that he had been spotted at the edge of the Red Sea, sporting a thick, fake beard and wildly waving a staff. MSNBC announced that "Hosni Mubarak" can be rearranged to spell "Main Okra Bush." The NY Times announced that Mubarak's cabinet, who had collectively resigned yesterday, quickly un-resigned when they got an inter-office memo titled, "How To Prepare Your Private Parts For The Mummification Process."

Due to a garbled miscommunication, US Intelligence stormed dozens of Quilts 'R' Us outlets, hoping to root out clandestine cells associated with something called the Muslin Brotherhood.

And then, suddenly, Egypt's President changed his mind and resigned, possibly due to some bad egg salad. His hastily-appointed interim Vice President was named Hussein, which apparently happens a lot in the Middle East. Think of it as their 5,000-year-old equivalent to, oh, say, Wisconsin's "Bob."

And, given the kind of week it had been, within fifteen minutes, somebody tried to shoot him.

And, of course, fifteen seconds after *that*, everybody in "official" Washington had to log their "professional" comments.

Stern-Faced But Benign On-Air News Personality: "Your comments on this assassination attempt directed at Egypt's new VP?"
Hillary: "I think that brings into sharp relief the challenges we face navigating this period."
Homeland Security: "The what? Who shot what who?"
Robert "Obviously" Gibbs: "I'm obviously not going to get into, um, that is. We fully, um, to it."
President Barack "Bob" Obama: "I protected him with my force field. Rise, my people."
Vice President Joe "Bleep" Biden: "Hillary did it. And it's a big <bleep> deal."
News Personality: "Back to you, Biff."

Odd times, indeed. So let's review where things stood, at that point, here on our little blue marble.

In Wisconsin, thousands of benefit-challenged schoolteachers were in the capital city, Tel Aviv, standing outside, freezing, and yelling. In Egypt's capital city, Milwaukee, thousands of meat-challenged people who were not named Bob were standing outside, not freezing, but yelling anyway. Somewhere in a Bahrain hotel, the members of half a state legislature were still getting paid, and racking up huge trans-generational debt in the form of pay-per-view cable movies. And in schools all across Wisconsin, thousands of unmonitored students were going all "Lord of the Flies," eating fast food, shunning vegetables, texting words like "r" and "2", and generally rushing headlong towards a dumb-downed life of doubt, distrust and loathing.

But, like most things, it's not all gloom and doom. Dark cloud, silver lining, all that rot. Remember, Egypt's temporary leader is named Hussein.

See? How cool is that! So is ours!

And Egypt's Hussein is clever, too. Using some stashed billions that had been "liberated" from US foreign aid, Hussein bought a Cleanup & Restoration company, sprayed some of their clean-up chemicals all up and down the Nile, and now all is well again.

In Egypt. Not in Wisconsin.

US Foreign Aid -- Like It Never Even Happened.

Santa Cops A Plea

(America rushes to get out of 2010. Can you blame us?)

It began with a simple pre-Christmas TV interview. And after the smoke finally cleared in America, Congress had locked itself in the bathroom, Homeland Security had outlawed Boy Scouts as carry-on luggage, Santa was in custody, and cranberries had stormed the Vatican.

It was just intended to be a fluff piece: a slow-news-day slot-filler bunged together by the ratings-challenged NABCBS network. NABCBS news anchor, the perky and engaging Cokie "Geraldo" Stoppinhalfabolus, was interviewing the head of all US Intelligence, a nearly inert fellow bearing the high-salary title of DNI (Dim, Numb, Irrelevant). The DNI, who looks a lot like a man slowly recovering from a University of Wisconsin football homecoming weekend, is the civil servant ultimately responsible for keeping Americans safe at Starbucks' drive-thrus from disgruntled invaders based in third world countries, like Absurdistan and Florida.

NABCBS News: So what about this terrorist plot in London?

DNI: Yeah, right. Any bagels left?

NABCBS: No, seriously!

DNI: You mean THE London, over there in, um, whaddayacallit?

NABCBS: England?

He didn't know.

The coordinator of all American Intelligence efforts had no clue. You and I, we can't wear shoes for twenty consecutive minutes in an airport, but this DNI guy didn't know what every tax-paying, TV-watching, barefoot airport traveler already knew.

Obviously, this was very bad news - insultingly unprofessional, staggeringly expensive, ultimately useless. However, the government's response was as typical as it gets: colossal, misinformed overreaction.

Damage Control flunkies flooded the floodlights. Excuses were floated, blaming everything from "garbled communications" to global warming to George Bush. Members of Congress suited up, leapt in front of any camera that got within leaping range, flashed some teeth, and began spending money (aka "doing the people's business"). Meanwhile, America was just trying to have a holly, jolly Christmas, thank you very much.

Let's hit some of the holiday highlights:

- Janet Neapolitan, who's apparently in charge of Homeland Security for some country we don't live in, assured her country that Homeland Security is on the job, 364 days a year. By the end of the week, Joe Biden had leaked the day each year when Homeland Security is off.

- Internet chatter uncovered that jihadist Boy Scouts might attack a plane using a thermos. Due to a garbled communication, the director of US Intelligence pulled out his sidearm and killed a take-out order of hummus. New travel restrictions required that all Boy Scouts boarding a plane be sealed in a clear plastic bag.

- A pilot who filmed TSA security flaws was punished for his whistle-blowing. Internet bloggers were quick to point out the blatant double standard in calling him a "criminal." Over the past two years, the bloggers argued, if someone had spewed security secrets to the public and the press, we called that person "Vice President."

- A new Wii "Sports" device debuted as the hot gift item this Christmas. You stand on a little white pad, answer a few health questions about yourself, and then you just stand there for a while, while the Wii stares at you. Eventually, you break down and answer the health questions without lying, and then the Wii cheerfully leads you through several conditioning and coordination games, like Heading The Soccer Ball, Dodging The Playground Bully's Sharp Rocks, and Airport Security Pre-Holiday-Flight Gang-Frisk.

- The FBI arrested a man at the Miami airport after bullets in his checked luggage exploded. Due to a garbled communication, the head of US Intelligence outlawed all plaid suitcases and arrested several dozen Cuban sandwiches.

- Apparently, there was a logistics problem with a Polynesian voyaging society in Hawaii, and this crisis required some of your tax dollars. So Congress agreed to subsidize stem cell genetic research that created a more travel-savvy society, called Uninesians. These new creatures were immediately driven to an ACORN voter registration office, where they were given free health care and in-state tuition.

- Internet chatter uncovered a terrorist plot to attack us via our food supply. But then the terrorists noticed the garbage we were shoving into ourselves on our own, and the terrorists decided to just sit back and wait.

- Based on an FBI report leaked by a "Vice President," the 2009 Detroit Christmas Bomber didn't act alone. He had help. That means that other people were in his underwear. The head of US Intelligence responded by outlawing both fruit and looms.

- Apparently, there was a problem in New Jersey getting cranberries to breed, and this crisis required some of your tax dollars. So Congress agreed to fund the "Cranberries Are People, Too" spending initiative, providing funding for pajama-grams, some mulled wine and bog mood lighting, plus a stipend to purchase a recording of Fats Domino crooning "Blueberry Hill."

- According to a NORAD update, Santa Claus was spotted in India. Due to a garbled communication, the director of US Intelligence called for an air strike, successfully carpet-bombing some satin clothes in Indiana. Already facing ASPCA charges of "tiny reindeer abuse," Santa was hauled in for questioning in several South Florida home invasions.

- Internet chatter uncovered a garbled communication in South Carolina, which is a ridiculously redundant statement on many, many levels. Due to a glottal warbling, the director of US Intelligence attempted to place an encoded, back-channel phone call to Pyongyang, the capital of North Karolina.

- The Vatican went on record as being solidly against Congress' new spending initiative, "Condoms for Cranberries."
- Apparently, there was a problem with bovine tuberculosis in Minnesota, and this crisis required some of your tax dollars. So Congress provided funding to relocate all Minnesotan cows to rent-controlled condos in South Florida. Congress then reimbursed every rancher in Montana, because the funding committee had misspelled Minnesota.
- After his 1:15 news conference, and his 2:15 presser, and his 3:15 photo opp, President Shellac O'Drama held another media event at 4:15, just in case you forgot, since 3:15, what both sides of his chin look like. At the event, the President read some more stuff he either did, or said he did, or meant to do, which is the same thing. Afterwards, he flew off to accept history's first-ever Nobel Future Peace Prize.

And finally, the head of US Intelligence just happened to overhear at a hot dog stand about an embassy bombing in Rome, so he double-bagged his Boy Scouts and immediately booked a flight for Rome.

Rome, Georgia.

But let's give the DNI a break. The poor man has enough on his plate, just trying to get Charlotte back from North Korea.

Honey, Was That The Door?

(Short Attention Span Theater logs another milli-second)

Well, it took nearly ten years, but we finally found him. And captured him. And took him down.

And then we forgot his name.

That's right - if you watched very much TV last week, you very likely heard professional news announcements from several news-announcing professionals, professionally announcing the news that the United States had finally tracked down and caught The World's Most Wanted Man...

Obama bin Laden.

Of course, you and I know that "Obama bin Laden" was not his name. That's the name of our President! I think. Isn't it? Sure it is. You and I know that The World's Most Wanted Man was named Usama bin Hyden. Wasn't it? Or Ushuda bin Duckin. Or Orlando Al Jolson. I think. Or maybe it was al Haffa Hot Qaffi. Or was it ar' Sauna B Leakin?

It was odd to watch. After all this time, after all this effort, nobody in the news business could seem to remember the guy's name. Granted, his was not one of your standard, run-of-the-mill names, names we commonly, comfortably associate with "Father Knows Best" or "Leave it to Beaver," names like, say, Wally, or Jimbo. Or, say, Bill.

Or, say, Barack Hussein Osama.

But you would think that paid news professionals would know the difference between The World's Most Wanted Man and a bumbling guy in a suit whose experience is limited to organizing playgrounds and who can't say "I'm glad to be here" without reading from prepared notes and two or more teleprompters.

But let's not drag Donald Trump into this.

Name-fumbling aside, the news story was huge. The World's Most Wanted Man, who according to Pakistan was absolutely not in Pakistan, was found in Pakistan. Nobody inside Pakistan was surprised, except for the entire Pakistani government, all fourteen professional soldiers in the Pakistani military, and a disgruntled waiter at the local Kebabs 'R' Us. Nobody *outside* Pakistan was surprised except for Geraldo Rivera, who still held out hope that he would eventually find The World's Baddest Bad Guy in Aruba.

Pakistani officials, attempting to be helpful allies, immediately threatened the United States, daring us to ever do such a thing again. And that triggered an indignant response from a spokes-droid at the U.S. State Department, who instantly responded to this insult by doubling our annual foreign aid to Pakistan.

In Pakistan, the face-saving damage control and political spinning shot out of the gate. According to official Pakistani sources, The World's Most Wanted Man must have had a nearly supernatural gift for hiding in plain sight. However, according to leaks from unofficial sources (see "Joe Biden"), the fugitive hosted a wildly-popular weekly poker game, regularly sang at local karaoke bars, and consistently sported a neon-green t-shirt bearing the slogan, "Al Qaeda: Dig My Posse."

Furthermore, The World's Most Wanted Man was a standard fixture on a popular Pakistani cable channel (WADI), where he hosted the ratings-grabbing reality show, "Fatwa Knows Best."

But last week, the U.S. military finally closed in on the amazingly well-hidden Bad Guy after several hundred thousand reward-seeking informants spotted him reporting the local weather on KUSH-TV, guest-conducting the Pakistani Philharmonic, and taping more "car recall" public service announcements for Toyota.

Overall, the bold military campaign went off without a hitch. And afterwards, there was much to be learned from reviewing the transcripts of the Pentagon's insertion-and-possible-extraction operation. When our military team popped in for their visit, they recalled hearing much murmured giggling and feigned, histrionic hollering from behind the door of the "clandestine compound."

(Yeah. Right. "Clandestine compound," my west-leaning east nostril. Turns out this guy had been about as demure in Pakistan as Richard Simmons on an espresso binge in a remake of "Caligula.")

Finally (according to the military debrief), after several anxious seconds, the "target" answered the door, wearing nothing but a red flannel shirt, a "Bat Masterson" felt Stetson, and a pair of plum-colored vinyl chaps. Apparently, America's score-settlers had interrupted The World's Most Wanted Man, and several of his wives, in the middle of a raucous game of "Scolding The School Marm."

Cleverly comprehending that this was not his usual Chapati Pizza delivery dude, The World's Most Wanted Man grabbed a nearby wife, slapped his chaps on her, shoved her out into the downtown Hilton's hallway to face the strike force, and slammed the door.

Then, confident in his politically-protected Pakistani cloister, he settled back down in front of his coal-powered laptop, logged back in to his Facebook account, and continued to swap odd hat photos with Muammar Qaddafi.

For a minute.

A Salad for Samson

(Top o' the food chain, Ma! Top o' the food chain!)

Ever wonder which of Earth's cultures is the oldest? Nobody can say with a certainty, with the possible exception of Al Gore. Or maybe Dick Clark, who rated the early Earth 3 stars ("it's got a catchy circadian rhythm, but it's hard to dance on"), or Strom Thurmond (during the Big Bang, he was serving his second term in Congress).

But one thing's for certain. Never has a world civilization risen to prominence based on a salad bar.

Now, normally, this is a discussion topic that would fall into my broad category of "whatever." Personally, I don't care if you eat beans, or bark, or boric acid, or Baltimore. But here's what triggered my interest. Recently, some group had some guy call me, to ask me if I would consider giving up meat.

No.

No, I will not consider giving up meat. I'm very close, however, to giving up answering the phone.

But give up meat? No. On this point, I'm going with my ancestors.

Despite all the endless attempts lately (by people I've never met) to manage my diet, there's one thing that's not debatable. Wherever we look throughout the broad sweep of history - from first rib to fig leaves - from mud to mating to mauling to monastery to mojo to motivational meetings - if there were people surviving, anywhere along the historical timeline, we can be sure of one thing: there was a sandwich involved.

There was meat on the menu.

We're guys. We go find stuff, we hit it, and if possible, we eat it. It's what we do. Maybe you've heard the term? Hunter-Gatherer? (current year's tax liability, addressed by lines 3a-6b on the IRS Schedule C itemized deduction worksheet, assuming you're a non-clergy Hunter-Gatherer with less than four pairs of white patent leather shoes)

It's what we do. Nobody invented the spear so they could better bring down a graceful grapefruit as it bounded across the African Kalahari. Robin Hood and The Boys didn't tease a Sheriff's fury by lobbing arrows at apples in Sherwood. Ugh, son of Ugh, didn't bother to figure out how to get a fire started by rubbing two Boy Scouts together, just so he could heat up some chick peas.

We may never know, of course, which group of us was the first group of us. The Egyptian dynasty is certainly a candidate for "The Civilizations of Earth, Chapter One." And so is the

Chinese empire, as well as the "Dream Time" aboriginal culture of Australia.

In many ways, the Egyptians were ahead of their time. Egyptian men wore skirts, sandals and eyeliner. And Egyptian women, to prove some kind of neurotic Fertile-Crescent-Female-type point, would seduce foreign rulers and then run around grabbing poisonous snakes. Furthermore, from decades of movies, we know that all Egyptian women looked like Elizabeth Taylor and all Egyptian men looked like Yul Brynner. (Okay, there was that one guy who looked like Edward G. Robinson. But he was fed to the locusts because he refused to wear eyeliner.)

Since we want to be historically accurate, or at least funny, we should note the historical possibility that Egyptian men applied eyeliner to only one eye. We think. We don't really know. After all, all extant Egyptian art features Egyptian citizens looking to the left or the right - never directly ahead. For some reason, we never get to see more than one Egyptian eye at a time. So we can't ever be sure what they were up to on the other side of their heads.

It's as if all Egyptians had their portraits painted from a chariot in the next lane, or while in line outside a trendy Cairo disco.

In fact, everybody in ancient Egyptian art is standing around like a very young Barack Obama, back in the days when he could only afford one teleprompter.

Odd eyeballs notwithstanding, the Egyptians clearly foresaw the cinematic potential of wrapping dead guys in cloth, with the dead guys' teeth somehow grinning through the cloth, so that, two thousand years later, the understandably furious dead guys could come back to life, hit stuff and if possible, eat it. Just peel away the dusty wrappers, snarl a bit, lob a few million scarab beetles around, and co-star in Brendan Fraser movies. Maybe that's what they were all staring at: box office receipts.

Plus, all other historical contributions aside, let's not forget that it was the Egyptians who invented the pyramid scheme.

As challengers to the Egyptians' claim of primacy, the Phoenicians have been around for a while, too, but nobody can seem to offer a clear explanation as to how they managed to get to Arizona in the first place. Still and yet, they've been a fixture for some time, as evidenced by that classic Glen Campbell tune, "By The Time I Get To Phoenicia," and the many hilarious references in the collected pre-Catskills comedy scrolls of that Sodom-based stand-up comic, Sid "Uncle Miltie" Lot.

"I just flew in from Sidon, and boy, are my arms Tyre'd!"
"Take a pinch of my wife! Please!"

My point is simple: guys want protein. Always have. From the protean time before our species had even invented the word "time" ... or, for that matter, the words "protean" or "invented" or "iPhone Sudoku app" ... guys have looked past arugula and longed for all-beef patty.

But some people won't stand for it. "Tsk tsk. Meat is unhealthy," they say, although it's not really possible to say "tsk."

Some people are like that. Always in your business. Here's what I think happens to some people: after years and years of watching network television and eating products that spell "cheese" with a Z, they finally manage to construct a thought, and then they start to simmer. They can't stand it. They can't stop until everybody else has that thought, too.

I think the original Yiddish term was "Nosy Parker."

So, look. Stop it. Leave us alone. This is what guys do. At least we don't flit about the Sahara with only one eye made up, flirting with Roman emperors and leaping on adders. Do we? Hmmm?

And let's keep this in mind, too: we don't hear about Samson accomplishing very much with the "jawbone of a three-bean salad." Do we?

Hmmm?

Life Irritates Art

(A bird in the hand is still not safe from George Bush.)

Tonight, the world can sleep.

Interestingly, it was the blue-stained turtle doves that finally broke the case and led to the downfall of Interpol's most wanted bad guy, George "Dubya" Bush.

And tonight, the world can rest easy. Let's review the timeline.

First, we learned that over ten thousand red-winged blackbirds in Arkansas had all died, at the same time, if you can believe that a coroner in Arkansas ran rapid forensics on ten thousand birds.

Within the hour, FlocksNews and the other twenty-four-hour-a-day news channels were blasting out news alerts. FlocksNews cut into their fascinating three-part series on an alarming rise in cat obesity, generated a new set of we're-all-going-to-die public-alarm panic graphics, and sat-linked to their local Arkansas TV/newspaper affiliate, KRAK. ("KRAK-TV. We cover the news forwards, and, um ... uh ... and, uh ... that other way, too.")

A reporter who often works for KRAK interviewed a partially-dressed resident who was in his front yard, cooking something on a stick. "They just went crazy. Just flyin' into once another and droppin' outer sky like manner from heh-uhm. Why, I kernt bag 'em fass enough. I had to call my wife," stated the resident, a light reader who only buys KRAK on the weekends.

An alert blogger who gets KRAK daily noted that, at or near the time of the fowl incident, George "Dubya" Bush had been spotted at his Texas ranch, smiling that way he does.

Several scientists from NASA who, thanks to budget cuts, had absolutely nothing going on, suggested that the plummet-happy birds may have been spooked by fireworks, or an Arkansas bimbo eruption. Ornithologists had no comment to make, since none of these birds, technically, were Orniths.

According to another expert, the blackbirds may have been roosting for the night, were somehow startled into flight, and at that point the birds all ran into each other. As the segment producer at FlocksNews later noted, this is the kind of expert you really want to avoid.

Then things really started getting weird. A report crossed the news wire, describing a similarly large bird dropping in Louisiana, and then another in Florida (the dead birds that landed in Palm Beach County had to be recounted).

An alert conspiracy theorist noted that, earlier in the day, Dubya had called his brother, Jeb, in Florida, and had then pointed up in the sky, smiling, you know, that way he does.

One Florida non-resident (which is redundant) cited a high incidence of "blunt force trauma," but an alert reporter soon discovered that the drug dealer (aka: "undocumented transient pharmacist") was simply referring to a road rage incident at a North Miami mall.

All across America, copycat theories were tossed around, particularly among people who, in the mid-morning, were already drinking heavily. Were these events somehow related? Had the Florida birds been watching FlocksNews? Did birds in Florida have cable?

Suddenly, the plot thickened. The list of usual suspects got unusual. Off the coast of Maryland, over two million bottom-feeding drum fish went belly-up, if you can believe that Maryland has an off-shore bottom-feeding coroner's office. Next, large numbers of New Zealand snapper began bay-bobbing. Not to be outdone by capitalist fauna, Vietnamese tilapia began beachheading like Niobe after lunch.

Next in the day's events, FlocksNews reported that Saudi Arabia had detained a vulture, which had been accused of being an Israeli spy. That has absolutely nothing to do with my story, but there's no way I'm missing the chance to say that.

Meanwhile, the modified behavior crisis spread to other species. The Santa Barbara skunk population exploded, and even in Santa Barbara, you just don't need exploding skunks. At the Memphis zoo, the pandas stopped mating and had to be temporarily banned from Beale Street blues clubs. One of the Thanksgiving turkeys that had previously been pardoned by President Obama scribbled a bitter note about "national emblems" and "bald eagles" and then committed suicide by deep-frying itself.

Scientists pointed out that bulk de-beastings such as these happened all the time. Long ago, you'll recall, all the dinosaurs vanished, around 3pm on a Thursday, after getting hit by a Bruce Willis movie. More recently, a quarter of a million ducks suddenly died one year in Canada after eating a bad oyster, but they were all reanimated after migrating to America to take advantage of quality health care.

As the news day went on, more birds croaked in Sweden and Denmark. Additional fish did the big sand suck in South Carolina and Brazil. Forty thousand crabs floated up in the United Kingdom, and over eight thousand turtle doves dropped to earth in Italy, with odd blue stains on their beaks.

Blue stains? Blue? Why blue?

Someone selling "get in touch with your inner child NOW" voodoo dolls blamed the massive Brazilian fish deaths on the oceanic equivalent of psychic trauma: last year, fish from Brazil had gone to Jim-Jones-Kool-Aid-Land, too, and this year's fish had simply not yet gotten over last year's gang-bladder-bloat.

Obviously, it was just a matter of time before an alert anonymous person mentioned the 2012 Mayans. And obviously, the person was a psychotic, potentially dangerous, utter moron. But, on the other hand, the guy *was* alert, so FlocksNews generated a new we're-all-going-to-die panic graphic and gave the whacko his own show.

Obviously.

In the meantime, an alert anagram artist, working with a seemingly unrelated collection of cereal box tops, deduced that the state of Arkansas did not, in fact, exist. He claimed Arkansas was just a very realistic CGI effect from "Chaws," an early Steven Spielberg movie about Midwest land sharks and shady real estate deals.

But for an alert revisionist historian at the George Soros Institute For Unadvanced Studies, something still nagged. Something about those blue stains on those post-trauma pre-trattoria turtle doves. And, after tossing facts aside and ducking incoming bales of money, the research team finally hit on the elusive relationship matrix.

Doves = Peace. Dubya hates peace, almost as much as he hates grandparents and clean air.

Blue = Blue State = Democrat. 'Nuff said.

So there it was. Dubya. The Jackal. The scourge of international law, busted and bagged.

Granted, for a brief moment, an alert Second Amendment hater blamed Dick Cheney instead of Dubya. But then someone else pointed out how unlikely that would be, given what happened the *last* time Dick Cheney tried to hit a bird with a gun.

And so, tonight, the world sleeps.

And as it turns out, the experts at FlocksNews were right. We *are* all going to die.

Eventually.

Saint Clement Has Second Thoughts

(Clothing makes the man...makes the man take a woman...to the Abbey)

I don't know if you were watching, but last week at a wedding in England, a hat made history. A "royal" showed up in public wearing something on her head too bizarre even for pomp and pageantry, and Scotland Yard really had no option.

They had to arrest the hat.

This was a head ornament so hideous, even that reigning goofy-hat-monster Muammar Qaddafi was overheard saying, "ibn al Crikey! That's one ugly hat."

Yes, last week, over a billion human-being-type earth people watched an upper-crusted couple of lovely British kids get hitched, despite their being caught up in some kind of pan-galactic Silly Hat conference. Meanwhile, here at home in America, our own self-anointed King continued to not prosecute the non-war we're not fighting against neither Qaddafi nor Libya, while our own Parliament of Putzes geared up for re-election by busily failing to address any of the nonexistent problems that are not resulting from our lack of no crushing debt whatsoever.

The royal wedding between Prince William ("Wild Bill Codex") Mountbatten-Windsor and Kate ("Kommoner") Middleton was staged in London's stunning, historic Westminster Abbey. It was something to see, if you remembered to wake up and see it; after all, the festivities kicked in around four in the morning (our time zone), which in my opinion was a pretty cruel joke. But I guess that's what the "mean" means in Greenwich "Mean" Time (GMT).

Five-thousand-guest weddings, food that has no actual food in it, and silly hats: these are some of the more visible royal traditions of the timeless British Empire ... traditions that, from an American time zone perspective, have being steadily traditioning along for one thousand years and five hours. (as adjusted for GMT)

Although we blindly keep insisting that we don't have any royalty in America, we Americans remain fascinated by the fairy-tale-like idea of it. Kings, queens, princes, princesses, parades, palaces, public executions. The pomp, the ceremony, the titles, the Tower imprisonments, the tax-exempt status. Succession, primogeniture, intrigue, incest. Nepotism, beheadings, hemophilia. Gout.

And the hats! Don't forget the hats. And at the royal wedding, hats were well-represented.

Were they ever.

There were hats here, hats there. Hats of fame and folly, hats of envy, ennui and empire. Hats concocted of such stuff as dreams are made on, hats ready to cry 'Havoc!' and let slip the dogs of war. Hats that hinted, and hats that whispered, and hats that beckoned, and hats that belched.

There were gravity-defying head-cluttering creations that must have required an epidermal epoxy treatment. These hats looked like the northern half of a ski chalet's roof, but covered with feathers, as if several eagles blew up over Aspen.

There were complex hats that could support their own ecosystem. Colossal hats that might have begun life at the end of an axle on a Caterpillar earth mover. Hats that could comfortably seat a party of six.

Some of the distaff wedding guests looked like they'd been side-swiped in the skull by some demented trash-can-lid pop artist, armed with a bruised pastel palette and an exhausted staple-gun.

And don't think it was just the women making overly-declarative fashion statements, either. The groom's father, Prince "Bonnie" Charles (full name: Pippin Charlemagne Mountbatten-Windsor Knot of Unisex, Duke of Whales), doddered in dressed like somebody in the front row of the photo shoot for the Beatles' *Sergeant Pepper* album. Best man and baby brother, Prince "Hal" Harry (Proxy Duke bar Chaz, Scepter Fodder Docent Needham), seemed costumed to audition for an off-Broadway remake of "Babes in Toyland." And the groom, Prince William (Wilberforce Space-Mounten, Lord Half-Mercy, Regent Regis of Philbin), showed up in an outfit that made him look like Michael Jackson, except darker.

But as wild as the hat group assemblage was, one member of the royal family took the prize. I forget her exact, entire name, but it was something like Camellia Estoppel Parker-Brothers Smythe-Dudley Phinger Bowls (she was with Bonnie Prince Pepper). What a head-helmet, this! This was a hat for the ages, a hat that wanted a considered, composed comment from Kipling. Her hat was so big, there were other hats in orbit around it.

How did things get to this? Well, because I am just the type of moron to do such a thing, I spent a little time researching the history of hats. And now, I'd like to share with you the fascinating history of hats.

Yes, I'd *like* to. And, if there *was* a fascinating history of hats, I would start sharing it immediately. But I can't.

Because there *is* no fascinating history of hats.

According to my research on the Internet (insert your own joke here), the very first hats were worn by cavemen. These primitive hats were not at all like the stadium-sized feather-and-felt helmets observed at the royal wedding. The first cavemen hats consisted of little more than mud, or sticks, or smaller, very submissive neighboring cavemen, tied together with straw or prehistoric bungee cords. These hats were worn for protection from the elements and to prevent injury from falling rocks, weapons, masonry, the occasional small animal, or even smaller, even more submissive neighboring cavemen ... all examples of things that were often thrown by larger, more advanced cavemen who had already invented tools (Homo Depot).

Now, how primitive cavemen were familiar with masonry at *all* is a mystery, much less so much masonry that they had to dodge it.

You have to wonder if it might have been Masons, in fact, not an asteroid, that killed off the dinosaurs. That, or global warming.

Or George Bush.

The first image of somebody wearing a hat made out of something other than somebody else comes from a tomb painting from Thebes. Thebes, of course, was a wildly successful clothing boutique in ancient Egypt, proudly serving both pre- and post-mummification customers, with convenient locations at most Nile exit-ramps.

In the 1500s, Milan became the place to go for a nice hat, and hatmakers became known as "milliners," because nobody could spell "hatmaker." After all , it *was* still the 1500s, and everybody was still a moron.

Did you know there's a patron saint of people who make felt hats? It's true. Saint Clement is the patron saint of felt hatmakers. I don't know what transpired, at what point in hat history, but apparently the felt hat union managed to get themselves in trouble deep enough to require intervention from the Vatican. (see "morons in the 1500s")

Then, as often happened in-between getting invaded, the French got involved. In the 1700s, French hatmakers (now known as "plumassiers") started adding feathers to hats. At one point, entire stuffed birds were used for skull decoration and were attached to the tops of people's heads. And the sad truth is that people actually paid money to have this nonsense affixed to their faces, because even though 200 perfectly good years had elapsed, everybody was still a moron.

In the early 1900s, American men and women began to tire of the whole hat hassle (along with self-respect and personal responsibility), causing Congress to amend the Constitution, thereby creating "casual Friday."

In the 50s and 60s, hats gave way to wigs and hairspray. (see "loss of self-respect") Rather than buy stuff to shove on and wear, women simply paid to have someone sculpt their heads. (see "morons in the 1500s") This bouffant-cum-aerosol craze caused Congress to amend the Constitution, and that's how the ozone layer became our fifty-first State.

And eventually, outrageous hats more or less disappeared from the American fashion scene until the 2008 Presidential Inauguration, when Aretha Franklin showed up wearing what looked like about two-thirds of a "Mutual of Omaha's Wild Kingdom" episode stapled to her scalp.

But last week, at the royal wedding, all rules were off and all Silly Hat records were shattered. Young Kate and William managed to tie the knot and slip off to the reception, but the world was watching the hats.

According to the Internet, the circumference of the average woman's head is twenty-two-and-a-half inches. By my reckoning, the circumference of the average hat inside Westminster Abbey last week was about eleven feet. (three hats couldn't fit through the Abbey's front doors at all)

And in admirable service to timeless tradition, at least four hundred selfless pheasants gave their lives. Stiff upper beak, eh, what?

I don't know, but maybe there's a patron saint for pheasants. Maybe Saint Clement can make a call.

Midnight in the Axis of Good and Evil

(On fashion, firepower, and finding a decent agnostic cheeseburger)

The Far East. The Mideast. The Midwest. The West Wing.

We've lots to discuss, but we're desperately short on time. See, some expert is claiming that our "2012" math was wrong when we analyzed the Mayan calendar, and the world has, in fact, already ended. (We know he's a serious scientist because his hair was uncombed and he had elbow patches sewn into his jacket.)

So let's get moving. If we don't look slippy, we may not even get a chance to blow ourselves up, before the Mayans beat us to it. No matter how hard we try. And we're trying hard.

Witness:

The news analysis from Japan continues to confuse. One expert from the University of Michigan says we should immediately evacuate the entire northern hemisphere, except for the campus of Notre Dame. Another expert says we should calm down: this is just a minimal disruption in a power-generation facility, and you get exposed to more radiation when you heat up a Hot Pocket. We know they're serious scientists because they were both smoking pipes, and one was wearing a white lab coat. (The lab coat had elbow patches sewn in.)

In the Middle East, Qaddafi appeared on TV, wearing a hat that looked like one of those gold slip-on shoes you see grandmothers wearing on cruise ships, or in Orlando retirement communities.

In Dayton, Ohio, some candidates for the Dayton police force kept failing the admissions test. So the US Department Of Justice (DOJ) forced the Dayton PD to hire the failing candidates anyway. In an unrelated story, Dayton gun shops noted a sharp uptick in personal firearm sales. Later that week, the DOJ forced the Dayton DMV to grant commercial drivers' licenses to candidates who had died while taking the driving exam.

In the Middle East, Qaddafi appeared on TV, wearing what looked to be an ebony bamboo steamer on his head.

After somebody borrowed a globe, the White House completed a Far East nuclear risk assessment, and then published several photos of people sitting around a table looking troubled. (We know they're troubled because they were pursing their lips and making little teepee shapes with their hands.) Following the assessment, the President of the United States (POTUS) assured Americans that we're safe. According to a statement he issued from his golf cart on the 7th fairway, Japan is "far away."

In Illinois, the DOJ forced prisons to incarcerate people who had been proven innocent. In an unrelated story, Congress then approved funding for a "recidivism research" grant at the University of Chicago.

In the Middle East, Qaddafi appeared on TV, dressed in something Yul Brynner might have worn as the King of Siam in "The King and I," if the King of Siam had attended a taxpayer-funded Gender Reorientation seminar for San Francisco city employees.

Overheard White House War Room Snippet

Nobel Prize-Winning Nuclear Expert: The radioactive material has a particularly low cross-section for thermal neutron capture, and it takes four neutron absorptions to become another fissile isotope and undergo fission.

POTUS: So what do you guys think? Louisville versus Kentucky? Or Duke?

The next morning, POTUS stood somewhere and read some stuff to America, apparently while he was watching a tennis match. He read some important stuff, from screens on both sides of the room, or net, or aisle, or topic, about what we might or might not do in Libya, or not. (We know it was important because he pinched his thumb and forefinger together several times.) He announced Step One of his one-step plan: send Hillary to Paris, in case Qaddafi should show up at a French hat store.

Japan revealed a major breakthrough in their containment plans, announcing that they had finally found a three-mile-long extension cord on eBay. In an unrelated story, France immediately surrendered to Japan.

In the Middle East, Qaddafi appeared on TV, wearing a deep taupe Star Wars sand creature robe and a pair of welding goggles.

After checking some approval polls, the White House announced their firm commitment to checking approval polls. From a sports bar between the front and back nine, POTUS told the United Nations to go handle Libya, and then he hopped on the family jet and headed for Rio. Immediately rising to the challenge, the UN promised to give Qaddafi a really, really angry look.

Overheard White House War Room Snippet
Nobel Prize-Winning Nuclear Expert: The material is particularly unsuited to recycling in a thermal reactor and would be better used in a fast reactor where it can be fissioned directly; however, its low cross-section means that relatively little of it will be transmuted during one cycle in a thermal reactor.
POTUS: They got ESPN in Brazil?

The DOJ forced thousands of Baltimore residents to watch tapes of Charlie Sheen interviews until they took their own lives. In an unrelated story, the White House then claimed victory for a drastic drop in the Baltimore murder rate.

In the Middle East, Qaddafi appeared on TV, wearing something that Michael Jackson might have worn, if he had been on the cover of the Beatles' "Sargent Pepper" album.

The Associated Press reported a "nuclear cloud" from Japan, heading for California, but several scientists at a pool bar in Rio assured everyone that the cloud's contents were a billion times below harmful levels. France immediately surrendered to Rio.

Congress, rushing to take off on yet another vacation, spent the billion.

Overheard White House War Room Snippet

Nobel Prize-Winning Nuclear Expert: The odd-mass isotopes have about a 3/4 chance of undergoing fission on capture of a thermal neutron and about a 1/4 chance of retaining the neutron. The proportion is low at low burn-up but increases nonlinearly.

POTUS, from Rio: Hey, anybody bring that globe? Cool. Let's play a game. Spin it, and wherever it stops, send Hillary there next.

The next day was St. Patrick's Day, so POTUS had a bowl of Lucky Charms and then entertained somebody from Ireland. During the day, he stood in several places and read several speeches, all including his signature line: "And that's why, as I've always said, let there be no mistake." Appearing with the Irish visitor, he pointed out that America has no better friend than (*insert country name here*), and reminded Americans of the rich history of green stuff.

As so often happens after a Thursday, the next day was Friday. POTUS had planned to take the family down to TGIF for a photo op and some low-carb smiling; however, the ACLU complained that a restaurant with the phrase "Thank God" in its name was a clear violation of the time-honored principle of the separation of church and steak. So, instead, POTUS invited some friends over to spend the night, and they're gonna stay up late, and tell ghost stories, and pump their hands under their arms to make little rude splatty noises, and giggle, and not wear socks.

Overheard Editorial Press Room Snippet
Me: Regarding the previous paragraph, please acknowledge and admire my restraint. When the ACLU nixed the restaurant visit, you cannot imagine how badly I wanted to type POTUS POUTS.
POTUS: *POUTS?* What does *POUTS* stand for? Somebody go call Rahm!

In the Middle East, Qaddafi appeared on TV, wearing a lush green, loose-fitting, après-pool-bar number and a tasteful tan paper hat that was straight out of a 1950's diner. Perhaps he was trying to convince POTUS that he's Irish.

On Saturday, an extremely rare outbreak of French Foreign Legionnaire's Disease killed 500,000 unemployed citizens at an Orlando career seminar. In an unrelated story, the White House then took credit for an improving economy, pointing to a half-million-worker drop in unemployment claims.

After some s'mores and their midday nap, the UN demanded a cease-fire in Libya, which Qaddafi honored for almost the whole afternoon. But, to be fair, he didn't own a "surrender" hat, and all the stores in Paris were out of stock. The UN immediately surrendered to France.

Overheard White House War Room Snippet
Nobel Prize-Winning Nuclear Expert: Ultimately, there is a chance either of those two fissile isotopes will fail to fission but instead absorb the fourth neutron, on the way to even heavier actinides.
POTUS: We got a tee time yet? Did Rahm call?

And finally, the DOJ forced the University of Notre Dame to grant diplomas to students who had flunked, or dropped out, or who think "Wuthering Heights" is a government housing project.

In the Middle East, Qaddafi appeared on TV, wearing a stunning Donna Karan azure A-line and offset brass epaulets, and threatened to hand out free automatic weapons to any citizen who agreed to take a stand for collective bargaining.

No, wait. That was the Wisconsin teachers' union.

France immediately surrendered to Wisconsin and, just in case, to Orlando.

And eBay.

Setting Up Your Own Non-Prophet

(Suppose you threw a super-nova and nobody came?)

Saturday, 21 May 2011. A beautiful, late-Spring day in America. All was well with the world.

Right up to the point where the world ended.

I'm sure you saw the guy on the news. In California (not Florida, for a change), some tin-foil-hat hop-head (not Governor Terminator, for a change) claimed that the world was definitely going to end on 21 May 2011. Definitely. No, really. This time, definitely.

True, the same Skull-With-A-Screen-Door character had made the same lame claim back in 1994, when he predicted that the world was definitely going to end *that* year, on 21 September. Without fail. Definitely. Of course, when he said it, he was prognosticating from a Napa Valley vat, hopping on a pogo stick and wearing a Ninja Turtle push-up bra.

Author's Note: for those of you who attended public school, or are members of the Wisconsin legislature, the world did *not*, in fact, end in 1994.

Meanwhile, all the way up to 21 May 2011, life in America trundled along as usual. I, personally, was getting used to having been thrust back into corporate life, I'd survived another weekly gauntlet of commutes, and I was on track to actually finish a carton of milk before the expiration date. Sixteen more Presidential hopefuls announced that they were announcing a plan to consider announcing a plan to form an exploratory committee to look into planning an exploratory committee. Gasoline had gotten so expensive that pumps had been modified to directly accept gold ingots. And yet another entirely-married Governor (yeah, him) got caught participating in extra-marital shenanigans or, as it's known in the South Carolina Governor's mansion, "hiking."

And then, suddenly, a clever Californian TV evangelist claimed that he had figured out a secret code in the Bible that clued him in to some breaking news, eschatologically speaking - the end of life as we know it, Saturday, 6pm, Eastern Standard Time.

Author's Note: I love Captain Bran-Brain's "Eastern time zone" bit. Such attention to detail! Leave it to a TV evangelist to schedule the apocalypse during prime time.

Actually, Mr. Dances With Imaginary Wolves says that the end only *begins* on 21 May. According to him, the *real* end officially ends on 21 October. (No word on the exact time, Eastern, Greenwich or otherwise.) As a sidebar, Mr. Chock-Full-O-Nuts warned that, between the beginning of the end in May and the big null in October, things are going to get ugly round these parts. The entire planet will pretty much turn into a great big Roland Emmerich disaster movie, starring Bruce Willis as President Hillary Clinton and Ben Affleck as a large meteor.

As you might imagine, some people heeded the dire predictions of Blunt Force Trauma Boy, and duly ran about, "yea, in exceeding silliness," emptying their bank accounts and stocking up on such canned goods as would survive the destruction of the entire physical Universe. Sales of beef jerky spiked. If you tried to point out to these people that Sergeant Musty Mounds Bar had been dead wrong once before, back in 1994, they'd hit you with their beef jerky.

Many similarly impressionable people turned to the internet for guidance which, if you think about it, is as good a sign as any that Gabriel's "Farewell Tour" horn section is warming up in some galactic green room. According to one internet site, "Doomsday will be unlike anything that anyone here on Earth has ever experienced before."

Stop it. Really? D'ya think? Worse than the *last* several Doomsdays?

And yes, citizens, you *can* buy an "I SURVIVED JUDGEMENT DAY 2011" t-shirt on the internet. And yes, "judgment" *is* misspelled, but since the world's nearly over for non-t-shirt owners, let's not niggle.

Author's Note: For some reason, the Total Destruction T-shirt website includes another ad alerting visitors to the five foods you should never eat if you don't want to get fat. I can't tell you what the five foods are, because to find out you have to order a free video for eleven bucks. I half-expected to see apocalyptic shipping options: "Order by 5:30pm Eastern to guarantee delivery before the extinction of all life on your planet! (some restrictions apply, offer not valid in Utah)"

Other, less gullible (and less likable) people took advantage of the situation (again, as you might imagine), and did their best to capitalize on the planetary paranoia, hoping to log some last-minute disgustingly selfish behavior before the cosmic curtain dropped. Suddenly, every product imaginable was offering a "lifetime warranty" and a "money-back guarantee," including day-old milk, and caskets, and vasectomies.

Weather personalities did away with the ten-day forecast, and predicted a very severe (but short) hurricane season. Garden centers reported a drastic drop in sales of perennials. Commodities traders sold short, or went long, or held, or clipped, or angled into the near flat for a buttonhook when the defense was showing blitz, or whatever it is they do in-between apparent ends of universes in which commodities traders don't have a vested fiduciary interest, if that's actually possible.

At hot-dish suppers across the American South, Baptists were observed eating their desserts first. Catholic charities didn't slow down a bit, and are still mailing me for donations. Oddly, though, I stopped getting mail from the Presbyterians and the Buddhists. Hmmm. Wonder what *they* know?

Things got so weird that ex-Presidential hopeful Donald Trump, America's favorite Follicle Monster, developed an honest-to-goodness sense of humor which, if you think about it, is as good a sign as any that the Four Horsemen are barreling down the home stretch. On his hit TV show, "Dancing With The Glee Club Survivor Stars Who Dissed The Celebrity Sorcerer's

Apprentice," His Trumpness looked an eager contestant in the eye and, what with the end of the world and everything, made the ultimate tease: "You're tenured."

Car dealers were the worst. After noting the "6pm Eastern" pronouncement by Admiral Aberration, some car dealers on the East Coast ran commercials in the Central Time Zone, just to get in that one extra hour's sales commission.

You may be wondering: how did the Cable Kook-Blanket Prophet-For-Profit come up with 21 May 2011? Easy. A simple combination of studied deduction, mathematical acumen and, I'm guessing, intravenous mescaline. Witness:

- The number 5 equals "atonement," the number 10 equals "completeness," and the number 17 equals "heaven." (source: Helen Thomas)
- Calculations begin on April 1, 33 AD. (source: eyewitness Strom Thurmond)
- The time between April 1, 33 AD and April 1, 2011 is 1,978 years.
- If 1,978 is multiplied by 365.2422 days (the number of days in a solar year), the result is 722,449. (source: one extremely bored grad student)
- The time between April 1 and May 21 is 51 days. (source: Sesame Street, Episode 208)
- 51 + 722,449 = 722,500. (source: my iPhone)
- 5 × 10 × 17, squared ... aka, atonement × completeness × heaven, squared ... also equals 722,500.
- Therefore, the world is ending Saturday at 6pm. Eastern. (source: mescaline)

See? Any questions? It's blisteringly simple.

Unless his calculations didn't compensate for Daylight Savings Time.

Hmmm. Hang on, I'll be right back. I better go get some milk.

ABOUT THE AUTHOR

Barry Parham is a freelance web developer and the author of humor columns, essays and short stories. He is a music fanatic, a 1981 graduate of the University of Georgia, and a self-described eco-narcissist.

Writing awards and recognitions earned by Parham include taking First Place in the November 2009 Writer's Circle Competition, several awards from HumorPress.com, and a plug by the official website of the Erma Bombeck Writers' Workshop.

Author's website:
http://www.pmWebs.com

The 'Straw-Heads' fan club at Facebook:
https://www.facebook.com/home.php?sk=group_233726315175

8587451R0

Made in the USA
Charleston, SC
24 June 2011